Abstract

Researchers have emphasized the importance of parental involvement in ensuring the educational success of children. Despite the recognised value, some stakeholders continue to struggle to leverage and sustain this partnership, which may encumber students' success. The ensuing chapters of this book seek to provide an understanding of the motivational factors influencing parental involvement in Jamaican high schools gleaned from a qualitative case study. Grounded in Epstein's school-family-community partnership model, this study unearthed some of the differences and similarities of parental involvement within high schools that were described as high performing and under performing schools and what informed those differences. Sixteen participants from 4 high schools were interviewed using a semi-structured interview guide. The data were analyzed thematically and interpreted against Epstein's theory. The findings of this study indicated that all stakeholders in a child's education had mutual interests and influences and an expressed desire to increase their involvement. The motivational factors driving their involvement varied however, from policies, beliefs, benefits and personal challenges; parental involvement also differed in quality and quantity across schools and requires creativity in design for greater involvement, accountability and impact. The strategic utility of these findings can assist in the creation of the home support engagements needed to remove the constraints impeding students and wider school success, thereby guiding students into successful directions, which is the thrust of a quality education system and the epitome of social change.

A THRUST FOR EQUITY AND QUALITY EDUCATION FOR ALL

EDUCATION'S MISSING LINK:
PARENTAL ENGAGEMENT

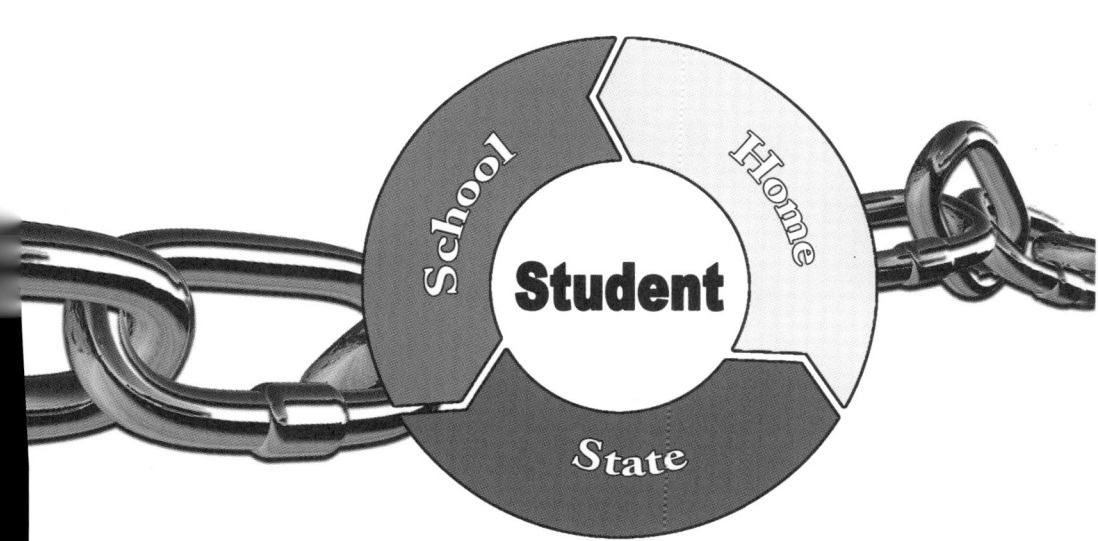

Dr. Kasan Troupe

LMH PUBLISHING LIMITED

© 2020 Dr. Kasan Troupe
First Edition
10 9 8 7 6 5 4 3 2 1

All rights reserved. No part of this book may be reproduced, stored in a retrieval system, or transmitted, in any form or by any means, electronic, mechanical, photocopying, recording, or otherwise, without the expressed written permission of the publisher or author.

If you have bought this book without a cover, you should be aware that it is "stolen" property. The publisher(s)/ author(s) have not received any payment for the "stripped" book, if it is printed without their authorization.

All LMH titles, imprints and distributed lines are available at special quantity discounts for bulk purchases for sales promotion, premiums, fund-raising, educational or institutional use.

Cover design: Roshane Mullings
Book design and formatting: Sanya Dockery

Published by: LMH Publishing Limited
Suite 10-11
Sagicor Industrial Park
7 Norman Road
Kingston C.S.O., Jamaica
Tel.: (876) 938-0005; Fax: (876) 759-8752
Email: lmhbookpublishing@cwjamaica.com
Website: www.lmhpublishing.com

Printed in the USA   ISBN:978-976-8245-85-4

NATIONAL LIBRARY OF JAMAICA CATALOGUING-IN-PUBLICATION DATA

Names: Troupe, Kasan, author.
Title: Education's missing link : parental engagement / Dr. Kasan
    Troupe.
Description: Kingston : LMH Publishing, 2020.
Identifiers: ISBN 9789768245854 (pbk).
Subjects: LCSH: Education – Parent participation – Jamaica. |
    Educational accountability – Jamaica. | Motivation in education
    – Jamaica. | Home and school – Jamaica.
Classification: DDC 371.192 -- dc23.

Contents

List of Tables..viii
List of Figures..viii

Section 1: The Problem 1
    Introduction 1
    The Local Problem..2
    Rationale 4
    Evidence of the Problem from the Professional
        Literature 6
    Definition of Terms 7
    Significance of the Study 8
    Guiding/Research Question 10
    Review of the Literature 11
    Conceptual Framework 11
    Review of the Broader Problem 12
    Summary 20
Section 2: The Methodology 21
    Introduction 21
    Qualitative Research Design and Approach 22
    Participants 23
    Data Collection 24

Data Analysis	25
Data Analysis and Findings	26
Description of the Schools	26
Themes Emerging from the Data	27
Judgments about Stakeholders' Involvement in Home Support Engagements	28
Pervasive Categories of Home Support Engagements	31
Daring Boundaries for Home Support Engagements	32
Connotations Defining Stakeholders' Behavior	34
Engaged Interactions in Schools	36
Barriers and Bridges Impacting Home Support Engagements	42
The Dynamics of Stewardship of Home Support Engagements	45
The Accountability Dilemma	47
Insights from the Findings	50
Shared Meanings of Home Support Engagements	51
Shared Value for Home Support Engagements	52
Varied Stewards and Number of Home Support Engagements in Schools	53
Home Support Catalysts	55
Redefining Methods of Home Support Engagements	57
Accountability for Home Support Engagements	60
Summary	62
Section 3: The Project	63
Introduction	63
Policy Background	64
Review of Literature	66
Redefining Home School Engagement	69
Incentivization of Home Support Engagements	70
Policy Description	73

Policy Implementation 76
Implementation Plan - Stage 1: Consultation 76
Implementation Plan - Stage 2: Crafting the Budget 81
Implementation Plan - Stage 3: Organizing the
 Systems 81
Implementation Plan - Stage 4: Launch of the Program 85
Implementation Plan - Stage 5: Policy Monitoring
 and Evaluation...85
Implementation Plan - Stage 6: Celebrations and
 Awards 86
Policy Implications 88
Section 4: Reflection 91
Reflection 91

Recommendations 95

References 99

LIST OF TABLES

Table 1. National Education Inspectorate Assessment Report of the State of Students' Performance in 205 Schools in Jamaica 5

Table 2. Demographics of the Research Participants 24

Table 3. Description of the Schools 28

Table 4. Types and Number of Home Support Engagements in the Categories of Parenting, Communicating and Volunteering in Each School 39

Table 5. Types and Number of Home Support Engagements in the Categories of Learning at Home, Decision Making and Collaborating in Each School 40

Table 6. Home School Incentive Program 75

Table 7. Incentive Chart 77

Table 8. Home Support Home-Based Incentive Program 78

LIST OF FIGURES

Figure 1. Parents' perceptions of the level of support they and other stakeholders give to home support engagements 29

Figure 2. Teachers' perceptions of the level of support they and other stakeholders give to home support engagements 30

Figure 3. Principals' perceptions of home support given by themselves and other stakeholders...31

Figure 4. Respondents' views on who should lead home support engagements..46

Figure 5. Stakeholders who should be held accountable for home support engagements 47

Figure 6. Proposed agenda of planning meeting 80

Figure 7. Parent involvement premium for a school with 500 students enrolled 82

Figure 8. Home school engagement incentives claim form 85

Figure 9. Home support engagement program evaluation form 87

Figure 10. Home school incentive award program 88

Section 1: The Problem

INTRODUCTION

Across the Jamaican landscape, several schools have been found to be ineffective or underperforming. Contributing factors to this state of affairs are lack of parent involvement in school-related activities and the absence of a framework to hold parents accountable (Caribbean Policy Research Institute [CAPRI], 2009). Based on a review of the education system in Jamaica, Davis (2004) recommended that the Jamaican government should promote greater involvement of parents in school-related activities to help drive improved student learning. Epstein (2014) espoused that though lacking, parental involvement was one of the most widely recognized factors that could impact a child's learning and Reynolds (2008) also found that children who did well were those whose parents were involved in their school. Since parental involvement has been recognized as a critical variable in the learning success of students, it would be of value to the educational improvement process to understand the motivations behind the parents' involvement. This qualitative case study sought to gain an understanding of the motivational factors influencing parental involvement within a climate of educational accountability in Jamaican high schools.

THE LOCAL PROBLEM

For many school leaders, the most difficult task has been to obtain the involvement of most parents in the education program of the institution. Though structures are established to facilitate parent involvement, including Parent Teachers' Association (PTA), parent teachers' conferences, text messaging communication plans, virtual notice boards and school websites among others, less than one third of the parents participate in these structured initiatives and have consequently reported that they were not fully aware of school requirements designed for optimal learning, especially when they are called about their children's acts of indiscipline. Teachers have been forced to double their efforts and make use of limited teaching time to deal with undesirable behaviours of students, a task that has become increasingly burdensome for them.

Despite schools having a specified and announced period during which students and parents are to collect textbooks, which are provided by the government at no cost to parents, principals have had to distribute textbooks to individual classes to ensure that each student collects their set of text. In some cases, principals have had to ensure that each class is assigned a class set so that teaching is not hampered by the frequent failure of students to carry their books to class. Further, while parents have shown a propensity to insulate themselves from involvement in the education process, a number are quick to be aggrieved when agreed disciplinary measures, which they failed to read in the school rules, are taken against their children for failure to do their homework, take their materials to class or just to obey the school rules. These aggrieved parents sometimes proffer false reports to the media, a number of which have sullied the school's reputation nationally and forced the administrative team to allocate time and other resources to undo the damage.

SECTION 1: THE PROBLEM

Within the wider local context, it was found from a commissioned review of the education system in Jamaica that partnership between home and school was weak; consequently, it was recommended that the Jamaican government promote greater involvement of parents in an effort to strengthen the link between home and school (Davis, 2004). The president of the National PTA of Jamaica reported that the attendance rate of parents to the parent teachers' meetings at most schools, stood at 20%-30%, and this figure decreases as the students progressed through the grades (Reynolds, 2008). Reynolds also opined that children who did well were those whose parents were involved in their school life, and so he amplified the call for parents to become more involved so as to improve students' performance. In the 2012 update on the government's educational transformation efforts, it was articulated that given the critical role played by PTAs, too many schools were without PTAs or had ineffective ones (Ministry of Education Supplement for Staff, 2012).

Findings from research established the fact that "ensuring accountability in education does not rest solely with the Ministry of Education and other school personnel, but also with parents and the communities in which the schools exist" (CAPRI, 2009, p.17). Therefore, the need to leverage the involvement of parents in the education process is central to the quest for improved student performance. Despite the general consensus amongst stakeholders that this is so, and though there are studies giving strong support for parental involvement, there is a dearth of literature illuminating the differential role and impact of home-school partnerships within Jamaican schools. For this reason, a qualitative case study was conducted to unearth some of the differences and similarities of parental involvement within high schools that were described based on national standards as high performing and underperforming schools, examine what informed these differences, and gain an understanding of the motivational factors influencing parental involvement within a climate of educational accountability in Jamaican high schools.

RATIONALE

Many of the leading discussions on education reform have focused on improving school success as part of the quest for educational accountability (Bennett-Conroy, 2012; Epstein, 2014; Hornby & Lafaele, 2011; Kabir & Akter, 2014; Merrill, Devine, Brown, & Brown, 2010). An evaluation of several schools in the United States showed that there was a drive for improved test scores, which were used in the monitoring of school performance (Hall & Ryan, 2011). A similar reform process is currently underway in Jamaica and continues to put increased pressure on schools to be more accountable for the quality education they provide to their students. According to Hamilton (2012), the National Education Inspectorate's (NEI) inspection reports of 130 Jamaican schools upended the state of affairs at many of the country's public schools and begged for significant improvements in school management and lesson delivery. The NEI's focus on eight key indicators of school effectiveness – leadership and management; teaching and learning; students' academic performance; students' academic progress; students' personal and social development; use of human and material resources; curriculum and enhancement programs; and students safety, security and wellbeing – found that of the 31 high schools inspected among the 130 schools, only 10 schools were found to be performing at the level of good and above (Hamilton, 2012). In subsequent reports on another 205 public schools, the NEI report composed by Dwyer (2013) revealed that 56% of the schools were rated as ineffective (p. 5), as shown in Table 1. Also, as indicated in Table 1 under the caption student attainment, the NEI report further revealed that 75% of the schools were performing below the national average. This finding underscores the level of failure that the education system has been experiencing over time.

SECTION 1: THE PROBLEM

Table 1

NEI Assessment Report of the State of Students' Performance in 205 Schools in Jamaica

Students' attainment	Percentage of schools	Students' progress	Percentage of schools
Above average	4%	Good	3%
Average	21%	Satisfactory	39%
Below average	75%	Unsatisfactory	56%
		Needs immediate support	2%

Note. Adapted from "National Education Inspectorate Chief Inspector Report," by M. Dwyer, 2013. Copyright 2013 by Ministry of Education.

Speid (2015) opined that the closure of 18 schools in Jamaica was significantly influenced by the lack of parental support for the children and the schools in the affected communities. Speid went so far as to suggest that in the quest for stakeholder accountability, parents should not be let off the hook and thus, efforts should be made to tighten the grip on delinquent parents to save other schools that might face closure in the near future. From a study conducted in Jamaica, it was found that it was the norm for parents to register students for entry into the school system and thereafter engage in minimal school-related activities until it is time for the sitting of exit examinations or graduation (Murphy, 2002).

Based on data found in one local school, of the 1,620 students enrolled, on average, only 300 parents attended the bimonthly PTA meetings. An average of 600 parents attended the annual parent teachers' conference, where individual students' progress reports were discussed and issued to parents. Only 10% of the parents in attendance reported having knowledge of when their children had assignments or the assessment policy of the school. Further, Thwaites (2014) stated that "while it is the responsibility of the state to provide the basic requirements, for effective education, partnerships are required with all segments of the society to ensure quality and equity in education" (p. 4). Therefore, there is a need to understand what accounts for an effective parent involvement framework locally.

Evidence of the Problem from the Professional Literature

According to Epstein (2014), a key part of educational partnership is the home support for learning outcomes. Emanating from the extensive research done on attitudes toward and implementation of parental involvement, it was concluded that parents' involvement in homework and parents' beliefs about education and academic expectations for children are a few of the most widely recognized factors that impact a child's learning and development, (Epstein, 1995, 2001, 2014). These findings have led to the convincing notion that parents' educational involvement clearly benefits children's learning and achievement. Similarly, Jeynes (2012) articulated that students tend not only to benefit more academically when their parents were involved but also that there was a significant positive relationship between parental involvement programs and the academic success of students across all grade levels. Jeynes also found that the length of the parent involvement program resulted in a positive effect. Pakter and Chen (2013) also postulated that there was a positive trajectory for students' performance when parents were involved, irrespective of whether students were disaggregated by age, ethnography, social economic status, or any other demographic factor.

The value of parental involvement to student academic outcomes has not only received the attention of school personnel, but also policy-makers who have advocated for parent inclusion in educational reform activities. This was notably delineated in the No Child Left Behind Act of 2001 (U.S. Department of Education, n.d.) and emphasized by the Partnership for Educational Revitalization in the Americas and the CAPRI (2012), which both stated that schools can increase student performance if parents are more involved in both student learning and school policy. The repeated call for parental involvement suggests that educators are far from achieving the successful engagement of parents in education. Therefore, to aid in the development of successful and authentic home-school partnerships, there needs to be a deeper exploration of the factors impacting home support engagements.

DEFINITION OF TERMS

Culture of accountability: A system where it is the norm for individuals to be held responsible for the educational outcomes of children within their charge through the application of established auditable measures (performance standards and clear consequences for meeting or not meeting those standards), which are used to inform, to reorient future actions and decisions, and to justify what is done in relation to educational outcomes (Ambrosio, 2013; Puryear & Moodey, 2007).

High performing schools: Those schools that received the rating of good or exceptionally high from the NEI, a government entity created to assess schools, monitor improvements in weak and failing schools and to ensure that appropriate remedial action is taken (NEI, 2008, 2014). According to the NEI (2014), a school that receives a rating of good or above has achieved the expected level or is exceptionally high in its educational performance and provisions.

High performing students: Those who receive overall averages of 80% and over in their end of year internal assessments in their schools (NEI, 2008, 2014).

Home support engagement: Though often defined and measured in multiple ways, home support engagement means, parents working together with the school to create "school-like opportunities, events, and programs that reinforce, recognize, and reward students for good progress, creativity, contributions, and excellence" (Epstein, 1995, p. 702). It is synonymous with the term *parent involvement*, which also speaks to parents playing a proactive role in the education of their children and includes all the school-planned or home-planned activities that parents may engage in at home and at school in support of their children's learning and academic success (Epstein, 1995, 2011; Fantuzzo, Tighe, & Childs, 2000).

Low performing students: Those who receive overall averages of 49% and below on their end of year internal assessments in their schools (NEI, 2008, 2014).

Motivation: The theory of motivation postulated by Maslow (1943) defined the term as a need or a goal that influences particular actions designed to satisfy that need. This definition is consistent with that of Coetsee (2003), who explained that motivation is the willingness of individuals or teams to exert effort to attain identified goals or satisfy individual needs.

Underperforming schools: Those schools that received the rating of unsatisfactory or needing immediate attention from the NEI, which means they are below the minimum level of acceptability for schools (NEI, 2008, 2014).

SIGNIFICANCE OF THE STUDY

This qualitative case study can be considered a significant endeavour in helping stakeholders in education to gain a more in-depth understanding of the motivational forces behind parents' involvement in the education process. The unearthing of the beliefs contributing to or preventing home support engagements in the school setting can help to inform the development of remediating efforts both at the local and policy levels. Educators can benefit from this information that might help them better quantify and qualify the design of home support programs locally. This information may also be used by them to achieve and measure equity and a sense of social justice in the national bid to achieve improved educational quality and accountability.

Though parents are described as integral to the socializing forces that determine their children's educational outcomes (Bennett-Conroy,

2012), their involvement does not get the audited attention in the accountability debate as the focus appears to be mainly on the performance of teachers and principals (CAPRI, 2009). In this regard, parents and parent support organizations can benefit from using the findings of this research to request funding support to set up parenting programs, to educate parents on what might work within their varying environments, and what changes they can make to improve students' learning. The insights from this study may also be used as the explanation or supporting details behind advocacy and behavior change campaigns within community groups. Students may also benefit from understanding the need for parents to get involved in their learning and may actively participate in the parental involvement process by encouraging their parents to get involved in partnerships. This could also increase the opportunities for them to succeed in their learning, as greater partnership may be leveraged.

Since the education system in Jamaica is currently undergoing a state-led transformation, the findings from this qualitative case study present timely ideas and recommendations that can then be further researched and implemented to improve performance outcomes at the local schools. Schools may use these findings to create policy documents and evaluation guides. They may also use the study results to determine if parental involvement standards are in existence; are appropriate and are being met; and whether remediation efforts are needed, and if they are needed, what form they may take and the cost to implement them.

Home support for students' learning may be vital to realizing true social change (Reeler, 2015). Reeler suggested that "social or individual change is not a cause and effect response but is the release of the inner and outer constraints that hold persons in a particular state" (p. 16). If persons can be supported to move those constraints, then they can move themselves into successful directions (Reeler, 2015). Both home and school need to work in tandem for children to maximize their full potential, thereby, removing the social, educational, psychological, and other constraints that prevent them from taking advantage of opportunities or from making developmental choices (Bennett-Conroy, 2012). Incorporation of the knowledge and insights gained from this qualitative case study may result in the enabling force that helps to remove the constraints of student learning and future success, thereby increasing the chances for students to progress towards their life goals.

The labelling of a low performing school as a *failing* school, oftentimes leads to a significant loss of financial resources, and the label of *failure* tends to demotivate staff and students. The improved practices to be garnered from this research can, therefore, be used to respond to the gaps in teaching pedagogy, guarantee a more efficient use of government resources, and motivate staff and students. These are all desirable outcomes that are important for the improvement of the education sector.

GUIDING/RESEARCH QUESTION

The effectiveness of school administrators and teachers has been judged by students' performance on standardized examinations as well as internal examinations. There is, however, growing evidence that underscores the importance of home support in the successful education of a child (Bennett-Conroy, 2012; Epstein, 2011; Kabir & Akter, 2014; LaRocque et al., 2011; Pakter & Chen, 2013; Thwaites, 2014). This evidence suggests that the quality score of a child is not just the responsibility of school personnel but also that of the parent. Therefore, in this qualitative case study, the following research question and subquestions were explored:

How do parents and educators perceive home support engagements in the schools with which they are associated and what are the motivational factors influencing their home support engagements?

Subquestions
1. How do perceptions of home support engagements differ amongst parents or educators of high performing schools and low performing schools??
2. How do perceptions of home support engagements differ amongst parents of high achievers and parents of underperformers?
3. What are the motivational factors impacting home support for school-related activities?

SECTION 1: THE PROBLEM

REVIEW OF THE LITERATURE

In an effort to convey a rich and insightful understanding of home-school engagements within a culture of accountability, the tenets of a number of theories and research studies were examined. The following subsections include the summary and synthesis of the key points posited about parental involvement.

CONCEPTUAL FRAMEWORK

This qualitative case study was grounded in the theory of overlapping spheres of influence, embodied in the school-family-community partnership model posited by Epstein (2014). According to Epstein, families should become school-like, and schools and communities have more family-like settings that may promote student learning and healthy development. Based on the model, the child should be at the center of the overlapping spheres and though there are actions germane to each sphere, education is one such activity that is an important part of each sphere and is best carried out through collaboration between and among the spheres (Epstein, 2014).

Epstein (2014) put forward a framework of 6 types of involvement that may be used to gain a deeper understanding of the level of connectedness between home and school: *parenting, communicating, volunteering, learning at home, decision making, and collaborating.* According to Epstein (2014) parenting is sometimes referred to as Type 1 involvement and relates to the establishment of home environments that provide the necessary support for children to fulfill their roles as students and includes all the activities in which parents engage to raise happy, healthy children who become capable students. Communicating is sometimes referred to as Type 2 involvement and this speaks to the various forms of school-to-home and home-to-school communication about school activities and the progress of students, which is vital to the quest for students' success (Epstein, 2014). Type 3 or volunteering, involves recruiting parents to volunteer their time or other resources in support of the realization of school initiatives (Epstein, 2014). Type 4 or learning at home, involves providing information and ideas to families about ways they can help their children at home with their homework and other curriculum-related activities which redound to a school-like family and encourage parents to interact with the school curriculum (Epstein, 2014). Decision making or Type 5 involvement, has to do with the inclusion of parents in school decisions, developing parent leaders and representatives, while Type 6 involvement, or collaborating, involves collaborating with the community or identifying and integrating resources from the community to strengthen school programs, family practices, and student development and success (Epstein, 2014).

The school-family-community partnership model posited by Epstein provided the empirical evidence needed to support the key variables of interest in this qualitative case study: parental involvement and school success. The model offered a guide for reaching a better understanding of the significance of parental involvement as well as the specific roles and the likely activities in which both parents and school personnel may engage to create successful students. The theory also offered a guide in the development of the data collection instruments and the questions to be explored to unearth the perceptions of key educational stakeholders about impactful home support engagements for students' learning. The model was also used to ground the interpretation of the insights of the research participants and was used as the foundation on which to build new learning.

REVIEW OF THE BROADER PROBLEM

There is a confluence of leading educational thinkers concerning the importance of parent involvement as a national imperative. The home and school are acclaimed as important sources of support for children's learning and development and, thus, when connections among these sources are facilitated, development is optimized for children (Semke & Sheridan, 2012). The lack of centrality given to this critical association is considered to be one of the biggest travesties of the educational process over the past 4 decades (Hornby & Lafaele, 2011). Beyond the common practice of simply sending students to school, parents are to get actively involved in their children's learning in a structured and sustained manner.

Measures of Home Support

Home support, referred to as parental involvement, has often been defined and measured in multiple ways that included activities that parents engaged in at home and school and the positive attitudes parents have toward their child's education, school, and teacher (Epstein, 1996; Kohl, Lengua, & McMahon, 2000; Topor, Keane, Shelton & Calkins, 2010). The multiple viewpoints have led to the postulations of similar, but different classifications of parental involvement activities. Hornby (2000) developed 8 types of parental involvement: communication, liaison, education, support, information, collaboration, resource and policy. Epstein (2001) 6 types of parental involvement are highly regarded: parenting, communication, learning at home, volunteering to perform school activities, decision making, and community collaboration. Parental involvement for the Chinese can be articulated in 4 types: parents' academically related supervisions, such as spending time checking homework or preparing their children for upcoming quizzes or difficult problems; television restrictions; communications about school activities; and providing resources (e.g., hiring tutors, or paying for after school programs; Wang, 2015).

In a bid to increase student performance, schools are asked to involve parents more in both student learning and school policy (Partnership for Educational Revitalization in the Americas & CAPRI, 2012). This call for parental involvement has led to extensive work on attitudes toward and implementation of parental involvement (Epstein, 1995, 2001, 2014; Kabir & Akter, 2014); parents' involvement in homework (Hoover-Dempsey et al., 2005,); and parents' beliefs about education and academic expectations for children (LaRocque et al., 2011). Findings from these research studies have proven that parental beliefs and school involvement practices have positively impacted students' academic performance. In support of these findings, Otter (2014) examined how family resources and parental involvement, measured as parental beliefs and parental practices, impacted students' learning and also found that all the variables were positively related with students' academic performance, which in turn proved to be a strong determinant of the level of education attained beyond compulsory education. The congruence found in these studies have cascaded into widespread advocacy for home support for school-related activities as the evidence showed marked improvement in children's learning when parents were involved.

Factors Influencing Home Support

The factors that have been found to influence how involved parents are in their children's education are cultural beliefs and attitudes toward parental involvement, social class and social economic status, the school environment, and expectations of parental involvement (Dove et al., 2015); as well as the inability to attend meetings due to lack of time or not having anything to contribute (Sheng, 2012). Okeke (2014) posited that some parents are not involved because they do not know how to get involved while others feel that they do not have the type of cultural capital that corresponds with practices of their children's schools and so they do not feel welcome by the school environment. Adamski, Fraser, and Peiro (2013) have also found that low levels of parental involvement have persisted because of the debilitating effects of low income, the prevalence of single parent families among ethnic groups with language barriers, and differences in beliefs. Malone (2015) contended that the culture of a community, home, or school can create a challenge for an agreed standard to be arrived at in relation to what is meant and enacted in terms of adequate home-school support.

The reality is that culture determines what values and traditions individuals embrace, their mindsets, and their mannerisms (Johnson,

2012). Due to the fact that there is no consensus across school and home settings about what home support includes, the variety of views available can result in little or no support for home support programs (Malone, 2015). For example, in the Turkish culture, parents are of the notion that teachers are part of the family and as a result, teachers are afforded the opportunity to develop personal relationships with the family (Isk-Ercan, 2010). However, the teachers who are not Turkish and lack the awareness of Turkish culture, according to Isk-Ercan, may not make the kind of personal contact that is welcomed by the culture even if the parents are educated or have high socioeconomic backgrounds.

Despite increasing attention to the topic of home-school partnerships, relatively little information is known about their use and effects across school settings (Semke & Sheridan, 2012). What is known, however, is that rural schools, for example, are challenged by special conditions that impact the availability and delivery of coordinated home-school partnerships. In 2015, 18 rural schools were closed in Jamaica, which Speid (2015) posited was influenced by the lack of parental support for the children and the schools in their communities and that efforts should be made to tighten the grip on delinquent parents to save other schools that might face closure in the near future.

The contextual realities – geography, socioeconomic challenges, and educational levels, among others – facing educators, have therefore heightened the need for research on home-school partnerships across school settings (Semke & Sheridan, 2012). While school-led accountability measures have had a powerful influence on student learning, they cannot be relied on totally for the improvement of student learning (Lund & Shanklin, 2011). Notwithstanding the importance of the application of the best pedagogy and the execution of adequate school-based accountability measures, the home must work with the school to achieve the best learning outcome in ways that are appropriate for each school and family setting (Lund & Shanklin, 2011).

Advocacy for Home Support

While educators worldwide have voiced opposition toward the use of standardized tests to determine school accountability, not many have opposed a collaborative approach between parents and school officials (McMahon, 2014). As such, schools are asked to involve parents more in both student learning and school policy as a means of improving student performance (Partnership for Educational Revitalization in the Americas & CAPRI, 2012). Similarly, Okeke (2014) postulated that there needs to be a national policy that explicitly explains what school principals, teachers and parents should be engaged in within and beyond the walls of the schools concerning their children's learning with special emphasis on the synergic relationship between home and school and its importance to the overall success of each student. Okeke further advocated for other activities within schools, such as games night, parents' evening, home visits, PTAs and parents' speech and competition nights.

Based on the sociocultural theories of learning, family-related factors are central to the academic performance of children (Vygotsky, 1978). This theory adds credence to the findings of Dashdolgor (2011) who found that parental involvement in school work done at home has been shown to improve students' understanding of what was taught and also was found to motivate students to learn more. According to the constructivists, learning does not end in the classrooms but extends to the home environment as well (Vygotsky, 1978). Therefore, beyond the common practice of simply sending students to school, parents should also get actively involved in their children's learning in structured ways, such as assisting with classwork, giving guest presentations at school, and aiding in the planning of school functions (Dove et al., 2015).

Impact of Home Support

Topor et al. (2010) found that increased parent involvement was significant when related to a child's increased perception of cognitive competence. Topor et al. also found that increased perceived cognitive competence was related to higher achievement test scores because the students knew more content and understood it better as measured by both standardized achievement test scores and the child's classroom academic performance. Pakter and Chen (2013) also found that "there was a positive correlation between students' success when parents were more involved, irrespective of the subgroup of students: be it by age, ethnography, social economic status, or any other demographic factor" (p. 354).

Contrary to the view that parental involvement positively correlates to student performance, there are few studies that differ in opinion. In studies conducted by Fan and Chen (2001) and Shumow and Miller (2001), it was found that parents' involvement in their children's education, negatively correlated with their children's test scores. Fan and Chen, found that parental involvement, in the form of volunteering at school, was not significant in its impact on academic performance. However, according to Pakter and Chen (2013) this might have occurred because the children were already failing, since parental involvement tended to be prompted by students' failures.

McMahon (2014) and LaRocque et al. (2011), however, have found that parents who were involved in their children's academics tended to act more empowered and often provided valuable support to teachers and schools, thereby, fostering better learning environments: a variable that may be critical to the lifelong success of students. The fact that the No Child Left Behind Act of 2001 (U.S. Department of Education, n.d.) stated that schools that are desirous of benefiting from the Title I funds must design an action plan to facilitate the inclusion of parental involvement in their schools, suggests that policy makers tend to be in support of the call for a tripartite approach amongst the state, schools and parents as a critical component in increasing student achievement (Topor et al., 2010). Reece, Staudt and Ogle (2013) argued that students, whose parents were involved in their schooling, experienced better academic outcomes, attended school more regularly and advanced to postsecondary education. They, therefore, opined that the potential for success of efforts to increase school engagement can be increased if the self-esteem and self-efficacy of parents are addressed. According to Reece et al., it is not that parents do not care about their involvement, but in some cases they may not possess the knowledge and the necessary skillset concerning how to become involved in their children's schooling.

While there is a clear consensus on the value of parental involvement, there is less consensus and knowledge concerning how it should look and how policymakers should be promoting it (Cavanagh, 2012). As a result, many parent engagement activities have been attempted, but there also tends to be an amplified call for some quality minimum engagement or a tracking system, which could be used as a guide for the accountability efforts of parents (CAPRI, 2009). The question is no longer whether there is a need for partnership (Lim, 2012), but what is the most strategic manner in which the partnership should unfold or be accomplished.

Implications

Extensive recognition has been given to the importance of parent involvement in a child's learning and development and models of involvement have also been posited to guide parental inclusion in education (Epstein, 2001; Hornsby, 2000; Wang, 2015). Though parents are described as integral to the socializing forces that determine their children's educational outcomes (Bennett-Conroy, 2012), their involvement does not get the audited attention in the accountability debate, as the focus appears to be mainly on teacher and principal performance. Also, there are no established baselines to assess parent involvement across school settings that could be used to guide parents in fulfilling their responsibilities as accountable stakeholders.

This qualitative case study unearthed the types of home support engagements that characterized high school performance within varying contexts and the motivational factors influencing home support engagements that are instructive to the parent involvement improvement process. In so doing, this study uncovered some of the debilitating beliefs that have prevented parents from getting involved in school-related activities and also presented some insights into possible remedial activities. Additionally, the exposed benefits of this qualitative case study have suggested new opportunities for research and policy development.

The project direction, based on the findings of this study, led to the development of a policy recommendation, a guide to qualify and quantify successful parent involvement endeavours in a culture of accountability. This guide can be used as an evaluation tool to assess the types of parent involvement that exists in local schools, thereby, providing data on current status in schools that could inform actions for remediation.

SUMMARY

The literature suggests a prevailing view that parent involvement is critical to the educational success of students. The literature also suggests some guiding frameworks for parental involvement. Though these have been repeatedly emphasized, school personnel continue to struggle to increase and sustain the involvement of parents. However, with limited local research on the strategies that have been effective in local schools as well as an understanding of the factors limiting or enabling parental involvement, the measure of the quality and quantity of parental involvement remains elusive, while the burden of accountability resides mostly with school personnel. The thorough understanding of what strategies work within urban or rural settings in high or low performing schools is therefore useful to the reform of the education system. To develop an in-depth understanding of these variables, a qualitative methodology was employed. The subsequent section therefore outlines the details of the methodology that was employed and how the data were analyzed. This includes the specific design that was followed, the justification for the design, a description of the sample, the methods used to engage the sample as well as to protect the safety and privacy of participants.

Section 2: The Methodology

INTRODUCTION

As I performed my duties as a principal of a high school, I became motivated to improve the quality of education in my school. The comments and questions broached by my supervisors, the teachers with whom I worked, as well as the students and parents whom I served heightened my interest in student improvement. The many reports of failing schools and the implied waste of public funds echoed by many in the media propelled me to gain more insights into matters concerning parental involvement in a climate of educational accountability in Jamaican high schools.

Therefore, the purpose of this study was to explore how parents and educators (principals and teachers) perceived home support engagements at their schools and the motivational factors driving both parents' and educators' involvement in such engagements. The guiding question for this study was: How do parents and educators perceive the home support engagements in the schools with which they are associated and what are the motivational factors influencing their home support engagements? In order to address this question, I also asked the following supplementary questions:

1. How do perceptions about home support engagements differ amongst parents/educators of high performing schools and low performing schools?
2. How do perceptions about home support differ amongst parents of high achievers and parents of underperformers?
3. What are the motivational factors impacting home support for school-related activities?

In this section, I will provide a detailed account of the research methods employed to investigate the raised questions. In doing so, I will also provide descriptions of the research design method, its justification, the setting, and sampling procedures. A description of the strategies that were utilized to protect the rights of the participants will also be outlined.

QUALITATIVE RESEARCH DESIGN AND APPROACH

The potential benefits that can be obtained from an understanding of the perceptions driving or hindering home-school engagements within a climate of accountability demanded a qualitative method of investigation, rather than a quantitative approach. According to Creswell (2012), qualitative research involves the exploration of a problem, which results in the development of a detailed understanding of a central phenomenon. In addition, qualitative research tends to focus on understanding naturally occurring settings and events, which may help develop an in-depth understanding of the issue under study (Creswell, 2012; Miles, Huberman & Saldana, 2014).

The aim of this qualitative case study was to unearth some of the differences and similarities of parental involvement within high schools that were described, based on national standards, as high performing and underperforming schools and to determine what informs these differences. The study also sought to understand the motivational factors influencing parental involvement within a climate of educational accountability in Jamaican high schools. Based on these purposes, the qualitative case study design emerged naturally from the research question and helped led to the understanding that there were many different understandings of the parental involvement, parental improvement programs and provided the opportunity for the central phenomenon to be inductively and explicitly understood through the gathering of thick and rich descriptions from the participants.

PARTICIPANTS

The schools in this study were purposefully selected from the population of high schools that have been recently (within the last 3 academic years) inspected and rated by the NEI, but the participants (parents, teachers, and principals) were randomly selected within each school to guard against any biases. To obtain a broadened perspective, 2 urban and 2 rural high schools in Jamaica were selected. The schools were purposefully selected based on the following criteria: (a) one urban and one rural high school that were considered to be performing at a standard of good or above according to the NEI and (b) one urban and one rural high school that were considered to be performing below an acceptable school standard and rated as unsatisfactory or needing immediate support according to the NEI.

The sample was selected using a stratified random selection process which ensured that the criteria of school leadership, gender perspectives, parents from varying grades and performance levels (based on their children's performance data), and teachers with over 5 years of experience were met. A sample size of 16 participants was obtained randomly and included in this number were the principal of each high school (to capture the perspective of school leaders) and one teacher (with over 5 years of experience) and two parents (from varying year groups; one whose child belongs to high performing group and one with a child from the low performing group). As seen in Table 2, of the 16 participants in the study, all were employed, with varying years of affiliation, and the leaders of the schools were all men. This sample size, which consisted of participants from various grade levels and school sites and ratings, increased the maximum variation and credibility of the study (see Merriam, 2009) as well as produced data saturation that effectively addressed the research questions.

Table 2

Demographics of the Research Participants

Participants	Gender		Years of School Affiliation	Employment Status
	Males	Females		
Principal	4	0	8-25 years	Employed
Teacher	2	2	9-15 years	Employed
Parent	4	4	2-12 years	Employed

DATA COLLECTION

The data collected from this qualitative case study was done primarily through face-to-face semi-structured interviews, with the principals, parents and teachers from the 4 selected high schools. A semi-structured interview was used because it allowed for the use of scripted and probing questions, which were necessary for in-depth understanding of the responses given by the participants (Creswell, 2012; Lodico et al., 2010). It also allowed one to glean descriptive information in the respondents' own words. The data unearthed perceptions of home support engagements in education, the motivations behind home support, and the types of home support engagements that are characteristic of acceptable standards of school success within the Jamaican context.

SECTION 2: THE METHODOLOGY

DATA ANALYSIS

The data gathered in this study were analyzed by combining, reducing, and deciphering the data with the intention to answer the research questions while engaging the following key steps:

- Thorough examination of the data collected;

- The systematic search for themes and categories;

- Elaboration and refinement of the categories;

- Search for relationships and themes among categories; and

- Simplifying and integrating data into a meaningful understanding of the phenomenon under study.

A detailed and integrated description on the participants and their perceptions were then composed. The ideas were later grouped by stakeholder groupings to obtain the views of each stakeholder group and how it compared or contrasted within and across groups. In so doing, the major and minor themes were identified and a descriptive phrase based on the major ideas explained in the responses of the participants was devised and used to thoroughly describe what was learnt from the data. The above steps were repeated until the research questions were answered and sufficient meaning extracted from the data.

The narrative was augmented with visual diagrams such as tables, charts, and graphs to represent the array of themes that emerged from the data analysis. Samples of quotes from the participants to build readers' confidence in the accurate representations of the meanings and perceptions articulated by the participants and to underscore the important points were included. The constant comparative technique and member checking to ensure the credibility, dependability and transferability of the data were engaged. Following the transcription of each interview, the information was presented to each interviewee to review for accuracy and to make corrections where necessary.

DATA ANALYSIS AND FINDINGS

The ensuing discourse represents the subjective body of shared insights of the 16 participants, who were interviewed for the study. Four major themes emerged as outlined in Table 3. These were captured in a descriptive narrative, making use of pseudonyms, and included substantial amounts of illustrative transcripts and analyses subsumed under several subthemes.

Description of the Schools

As seen in Table 3, Webly High School (pseudonym) is situated in urban Jamaica, while McDonald High School (pseudonym) is situated in rural Jamaica. Both institutions were inspected and ranked by the NEI as good. Though they were both ranked as good by the NEI, Webly High School is assigned students by the Ministry of Education who have earned 90% and over in the national school placement examination , while McDonald High School is assigned students who earn 70% and over in the same examination (Ministry of Education School Placement List, 2016). Webly High School was ranked as a higher performing school than McDonald High School (Ministry of Education School Placement List, 2016) and the standards of high and low performance were defined differently by both schools. At Webly High School, high performance was defined by an average of 80% and over, while it was 70% and over at McDonald High School. Likewise, low performance was defined as an average of 59% and below at Webly High, while it was 49% and below at McDonald High. All the participants from Webly High were aware of the ranking of the school by the NEI, while this differed at McDonald High. Ms. Pearl Reid (pseudonym), one of the parents, was not aware of the ranking of the school and it must be noted that this parent was the parent of a low performing student in that school.

James High School (pseudonym) is situated in urban Jamaica, while Spain High (pseudonym) is situated in rural Jamaica. Both institutions were inspected and ranked by the NEI as needs immediate support and unsatisfactory respectively. Though they were both ranked below the standard of good by the NEI, James High School was assigned students who earned between 20% - 60% in the national school placement examination while Spain High was assigned students who earned between 45%-70% in the same examination. This means that Spain High was ranked higher than James High (Ministry of Education School Placement List, 2016). However, the standards of high and low performance were defined similarly as 70% and over and 40% and below respectively.

Only the principals and the teachers (educators) of James High and Spain High Schools were aware of the rankings of the schools as well as how high and low performances were defined or measured by both schools. Both sets of parents shared that they did not know the NEI rankings of the schools and that they were unsure how high and low performances were defined in the schools they were associated with. The educators (principals and teachers) of all four schools, however, were found to be knowledgeable of the NEI rankings of their schools, as well as the descriptions of high and low performances in their schools.

Though there were 4 male and 4 female parents who were affiliated with their schools for 2-6 years, there was no notable gender difference in awareness levels, as outlined in Table 3. Both genders had gaps in their knowledge of their schools' contexts. Notwithstanding the gender of the parents, it was found that the parents of the schools ranked as good were aware of the ranking and the descriptions of high and low performances in their schools, while the parents of the unsatisfactory and below schools were unaware of the ranking of the schools and were unsure of the descriptions of high and low performances in the schools.

Themes Emerging from the Data

Four major themes emerged from the data and these were expounded on accordingly: Judgments and connotations that defined stakeholders' involvement in home support activities, bridges and barriers impacting home support engagements, the dynamics of stewardship of home support engagements, and the accountability dilemma.

Judgments About Stakeholders' Involvement in Home Support Engagements

Table 3

Description of the Schools

Role at the School	Age Range	Years of School Affiliation	School/Parish	School Rank	Description of High Performance	Description of Low Performance
Mark Walder 1	46-64	13	Webly High - A	Good	80% and over	60% and below
Keith James 2	31-45	10	Webly High - A	Good	80% and over	60% and below
Luke Johns 3	31-45	2	Webly High - A	Good	80% and over	60% and below
Sheree Myles 4	31-45	4	Webly High - A	Good	80% and over	60% and below
Marlie Small 1	46-64	8	McDonald High - B	Good	70% and over	49% and below
Kerry Gayle 2	31-45	12	McDonald High - B	Good	70% and over	49% and below
Miller Cole 3	31-45	6	McDonald High - B	Good	80% and over	49% and below
Pearl Reid 4	46-64	3	McDonald High - B	I do not know	80% and over	49% and below
Selvin Biggs 1	46-64	25	James High – A	Needs immediate support	70% and over	40% and below
Aston Tapper 2	46-64	15	James High – A	Needs immediate support	70% and over	40% and below
Gary Smart 3	31-45	3	James High – A	I do not know	I am not sure	40% and below
Sylvia Slack 4	31-45	4	James High – A	I do not know	I am not sure	40% and below
Ralph Reid 1	46-64	10	Spain - B	Unsatisfactory	70% and over	40% and below
Marcia Fitt 2	31-45	9	Spain - B	Unsatisfactory	70% and over	40% and below
Shari Rickets 3	18-30	3	Spain - B	Needs immediate support	I am not sure	40% and below
Andrew Bills 4	46-64	2	Spain - B	Needs immediate support	80% and over	I am not sure

Note.   Key: 1 – Principal, 2 – Teacher, 3 and 4 – Parents; A – Urban, B – Rural

SECTION 2: THE METHODOLOGY

Each stakeholder group was asked to share their perceptions of the support they and other stakeholders gave to their schools using a rating scale of 1 - 10 (1 being the lowest and 10 being the highest). Figure 1, shows the level of support parents believed that they gave in comparison to the support given by principals, other parents and teachers within the school that they were affiliated with. As seen in Figure 1, the general views of the parents in regards to their perceptions about their level of involvement ranged from a score of 4 - 6, while that from the wider parent body ranged from a low of 3 to a high of 9. In respect to the educators, the general view was that the support given by the principals ranged from a low of 5 to a high of 9, while that given by the teachers ranged generally from a low of 4 to a high of 6. Overall, the highest support was perceived to be given by principals and parents. Figure 1 further shows that the level of home support was perceived to be higher in the schools rated as good and above by the NEI.

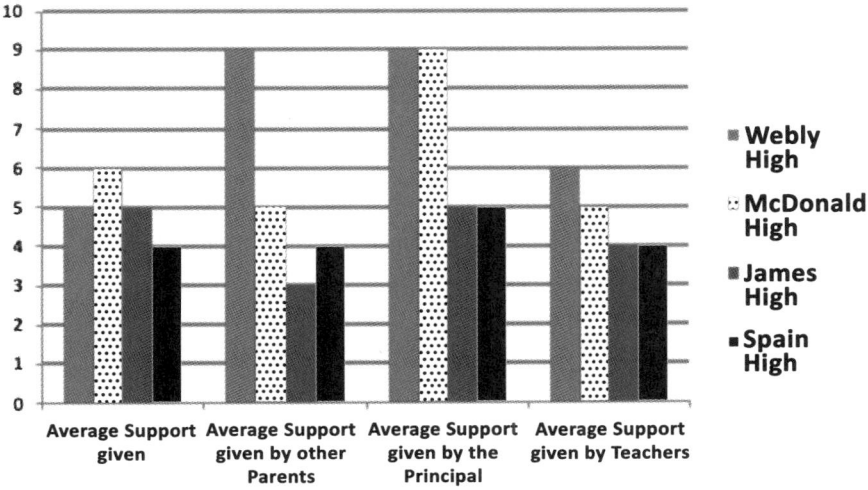

Figure 1. Parents' perceptions of the level of support they and other stakeholders give to home-support engagements.

As seen in Figure 2, the teachers' perceptions of the level of support they gave to home support engagements in their schools ranged from a low of 3 to a high of 6. They further perceived the support given by teachers in general to range from a low of 4 to a high of 7. On the other hand, parents were perceived to have given support ranging from a low of 4 to a high of 9, and that for principals ranged from a low of 5 to a high of 9. The teachers' perceptions of home support were highest for all stakeholders in Webly and McDonald High Schools (rated as good by the NEI) when compared to James and Spain High Schools, which were both rated as unsatisfactory and below by the NEI. Like the parents, the teachers also perceived that the principals and parents gave the most support across all 4 schools.

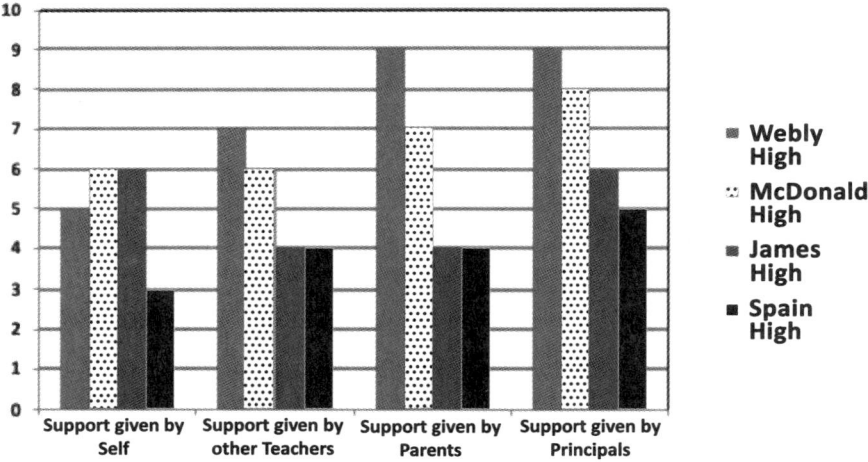

Figure 2. Teachers' perceptions of the level of support they and other stakeholders give to home-support engagements.

As seen in Figure 3, principals' perceptions of support given to home support engagements in their schools ranged from a low of 7 to a high of 9. In fact, this was higher than all other stakeholders as the parents were perceived to have given support ranging from a low of 3 to a high of 9 as seen in Figure 1, while teachers were perceived to

SECTION 2: THE METHODOLOGY

have given support ranging from a low of 3 to a high of 7 as seen in Figure 2. The highest support was seen in the schools rated as good by the NEI (Webly and McDonald High Schools) and, like the parents and teachers interviewed, the principals perceived that teachers have given the least support for home-support engagements within schools.

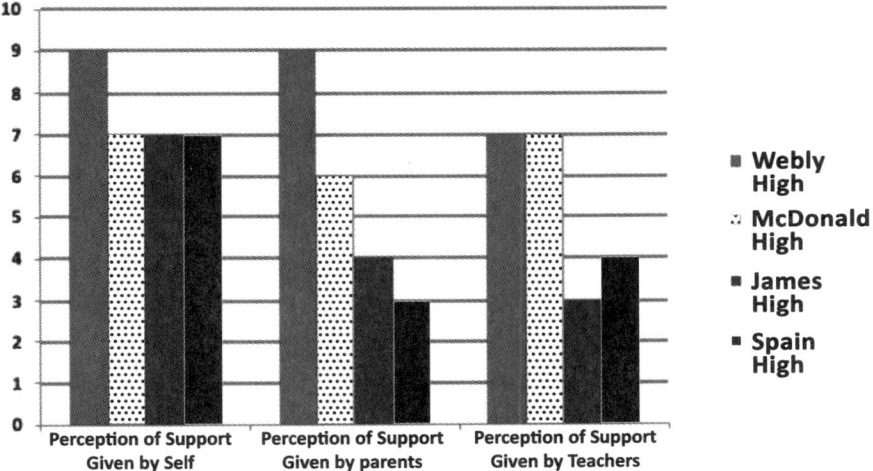

Figure 3. Principals' perceptions of the level of support they and other stakeholders give to home-support engagements.

Pervasive Categories of Home Support Engagements

The respondents articulated that there were some home-support engagements that should be in all schools as well as posited some minimum activities that all schools and parents should aim to facilitate. All respondents expressed that all school communities should endeavor to have as many activities under the 4 following pervasive categories: communicating, parenting, volunteering and decision making. The specific engagements that were shared were: an active PTA with at least 70% of the parents attending, parent consultation time to discuss students' performance, parent involvement through volunteerism in extracurricular activities and fundraising, systems to ensure homework is done, parenting skills sessions, decision making avenues regarding school programs, and two-way communication opportunities. It was also articulated that technology should be used to facilitate dialogue and feedback, as the traditional evening meeting approach hinders participation. Mr. Luke John (pseudonym), a parent of Webly High School, expressed the following:

> All schools must have an active PTA that is well supported with 70% and over of its parents attending. No good school can function well without this, as it is a key home-support engagement. Parents should also be involved in extracurricular activity like the sports and other clubs and societies. Their involvement makes a difference. Fundraising must be a part of the school and should be led by the parents. [The] school should make sure that parents supervise homework or to help schools develop homework centers.

Mr. Miller Cole (pseudonym), a parent of McDonald High also stated:
> All schools need an active PTA. One of the things though is that the teachers do not attend as often as they should. This is as a result of the time. I think the technology should be used to garner dialogue and feedback as the traditional evening meeting approach hinders teachers' participation. All schools should have an Open Day as well. Parents should see the place where the children spend most of their day, they should come in and tour the school and offer support. Parent and teachers in concert is a good thing to keep the children focused.

Daring Boundaries for Home Support Engagements

When asked whether there needed to be a minimum level of home support engagements from which parents should not be exempted and what those could be, all respondents agreed that there should be a minimum level of support that all parents must meet. In being specific, they expressed that parents should not be exempted from: attendance to PTA meetings and the parent consultation meetings where students' performance should be discussed. It was further suggested that each parent must attend at least one of these activities annually. Other minimum level activities were suggested, such as parents volunteering to lead extracurricular activities, systems to ensure students' homework are completed and students are prepared for school. A review of these minimum level engagements showed one dominant category of home-support engagement: communicating. This was reiterated by Sylvia Black (pseudonym) of James High School:

> Ahmm, minimum standard...okay, yes. I do believe that parents must attend a certain number of PTA meetings throughout the time of schooling, if it is even once per year. Parents must visit the school and have a word with their children's teachers at least one time per term. Parents must ensure that they prioritize, put what the child needs upfront. They should also ensure that homework is done and books are checked. Parents must check homework.

The respondents, in general, were of the view that schools planned, hosted home-support activities and shared expectations, but parents sometimes did not support them. When they were asked what improvements could be made in the area of home-support interactions, the ideas for improvement were situated in the category described by Epstein (2001) as parenting. It was suggested that efforts should be exerted in the area of improving parenting skills. It was the belief of the respondents that if parents are trained to love, value their children and be effective parents, then they would get more involved in home-support engagements. It was also articulated that if schools could be given more time and resources to do home visits, then parents and children would have more support. Some of the respondents also suggested an incentive scheme to motivate home-support engagements. In expounding on this, it was explained that home and schools could work out a points system for each agreed home support engagement that existed in their school and allow parents to earn points through their participation in each form of engagement. Parents should also be rewarded with medals or scholarships for their children based on how many points they earned. It was further said that a special grant could be given by the government to schools that operated parental involvement activities as a way of improving home-support engagements. Mr. Aston Tapper (pseudonym) of James High School expounded accordingly:

> As a way to improve home support engagements, I believe schools or even the government need to put in a points system. So, if parents met the minimum standard, students could benefit from a merit system, and the parents could be recognized for it as well. I think a reward system could motivate more involvement from parents. It does not need to be an expensive reward, it could be a picture posted in the school, a pen, a day out, a courtesy call with the prime minister among other things.

Connotations Defining Stakeholders' Behavior

In an effort to unearth respondents understanding of home support engagement, they were asked to proffer personal definitions of the terminology. The descriptions given were varied by stakeholder groups and were characterized by their engagements with their students/children and an overarching philosophy that informed the activities of engagement. It should be noted that the educators – principals and teachers – defined home-support engagement in a similar manner. They described it as all stakeholders working together to support student success in school. In giving more depth, they further explained that it entailed what the principals, teachers, government and parents did to support students, such as ensuring students are sent to schools and do their homework; providing resources and ensuring that students make use of these resources (books and other school supplies); providing funding for school improvement; attendance at school functions/activities, and volunteering to ensure the success of school activities. This showed an understanding of home-support engagement from a tripartite approach, involving the government, the school, and the

SECTION 2: THE METHODOLOGY

home. In expanding their understanding of home-support engagement, it was also shared that the number of activities that existed in a school that included parents' participation was a sign of how the principal viewed home-support engagement. It was purported that as the leader of the school, the principal is the main person who provided the cues for others to follow.

Parents on the other hand spoke mostly of home-support engagement from an emotional stand point. They saw it as the demonstration of love and encouragement that parents gave to their children to ensure they did well as students. According to the parent respondents, participating in school activities such as meetings, fundraising and buying school supplies showed how much they cared about their children's educational success. Mr. Luke Johns (pseudonym) of Webly High expounded by saying:

> Home-support engagement for me means buying the books, preparing my children for school and also being there to provide the love and support for them. It involves parents being consistent, aware of what is going on in school, letting their children know that they will attend school activities and will be checking on them. It is the physical presence of the parent at school as well as the love they show at home. The thing is, if the students' physical and psychological needs are met, they will do well in school. Students will not function well if they do not feel loved or cared for.

In support of the above, the respondents further elucidated on the evidence that they would use to determine if home-support engagements were being practiced in their schools and the responses were similar across stakeholder groups and typified the following: the establishment or presence of PTAs, attendance at PTAs by principals and teachers; attendance at parent teachers' conferences; the number of parents who volunteer to support school activities like clubs, sports, festivals among others; the funding support given by parents; the interest shown in the academic ranking of students and the school by parents;

and how students are prepared for school (e.g., whether they have correct uniforms, required books and other supplies), and whether the children complete homework and adhere to school rules.

In an attempt to explore this further, the respondents all agreed that home-support engagements were very important as they benefitted all persons involved by ensuring that students are successful in learning and, by extension, the school improves in ranking and earns stakeholder support more easily. According to the respondents, parents are afforded the opportunity to be proud because the job prospects of their children were increased when they did well in school. Though everyone benefits from home-support engagements, the respondents unanimously declared that it was the students who benefitted the most from home-support engagements. It was also strongly reiterated that no one stakeholder can ensure an effective home-support program, but rather that it was better done through a partnership. According to Mr. Mark Walder (pseudonym) of Webly High:

> Without home-support engagements the school and students cannot succeed. It cannot be left to the teachers alone, we need the various stakeholders. The PTA is extremely important as it creates the opportunity for all to give support to programs, students who cannot afford school fees, funding support for the development of teachers, the main medium for parents to give feedback and become aware of what is happening. Everything cannot be done at school; we need the parents' support.

Engaged Interactions in Schools

Based on the data gleaned from the survey and the semi-structured interviews, it was found that though there was unanimous agreement that home support engagements were important for student and school success, the levels of involvement, types of involvement, as well as the lead organizers of home-support programs varied across schools. In the schools that were rated as good by the NEI, home-support engagements and participation were far greater (see Tables

3, 4 and 5), educators and parents were aware of the ranking of the schools by the NEI, how quality student performance was defined, and the lead implementers of engagement activities were principals and parents.

As seen in Tables 4 and 5, the types of home-support engagements, as found in each school, were reflective of the 6 types of parent involvement proposed by Epstein (2001). All the proposed categories of home-support engagements were present in all 4 schools, but the number of activities and the level of support given varied across schools. All the schools were found to have PTAs, however, the difference in parental support at PTA meetings ranged from a low of 30% to 90% and the schools rated as good boasted the higher percentage of support. Whilst the parents in the schools ranked as good could fluently share the activities that took place in their schools, the parents of the low ranking schools struggled to do the same.

Based on Table 4, all the schools offered parenting seminars under the category of parenting, aimed at improving parenting skills and this is normally done in the month of November, which is celebrated annually as National Parent Month. Webly High was the only school that offered parenting training annually in the month of September for all new parents, to orientate them into the practices that they should inculcate to ensure their children are successful. It must be noted too that this seminar is organized and led by the parent body. Under the category of communication, several activities were found in common. All schools operated a PTA, but Webly and McDonald High Schools reported a higher attendance rate by parents than James and Spain High Schools. Other similar activities included parent teacher conferences, prize giving ceremonies for students, communication systems – text messaging, emails, website and WhatsApp platforms. Webly High was found to have several more communication activities that did not exist in the other schools; namely term meetings with parents, which were convened by teachers, and a weekly scheduled meeting with the principal. Additionally, parents who wished to dialogue with the principal without an appointment, were accommodated.

In the category of volunteering, similar activities were found across all schools. Some of these included parents volunteering as managers of clubs and societies, mentors, leaders of planning committees such as fundraisers, teachers' day events, welfare activities and other school functions. Webly High was found to have parents volunteering to teach in the absence of teachers, and to present at conferences designed for students, parents and teachers. With respect to learning at home, all schools were found to do the least number of activities in this category. These were limited to sharing tips on what parents can do to help their children to learn. This activity was led mostly by school personnel and, in some cases, by parent leaders. At Webly High, however, there were some differences: parents were provided with curriculum guides and the course outline for each subject area so that they could acquaint themselves with what was being done on a weekly basis at the school. According to the principal of Webly High School, Mr. Mark Walder:

> Nothing was done deliberately to teach the parents the subject content, but the parents we have seek external or additional support for their children if they are failing and so we have never really seen it as an area to improve on. However, now that I think about it, probably it is an area we could improve on for the future.

In the category of decision making, all the schools had a similar framework in place. The president of each PTA is a member of the school board and the subcommittees that govern the school. The PTA executive members meet monthly to discuss home-support engagements and posit and implement recommendations, such as those relating to school rules, homework policy, lunch menu and sport offerings.

There were some variations at Webly High School. In addition to those mentioned, Webly High's PTA leaders met monthly with teachers to discuss policies, school rules and suggestions for improvement and the parents agitated for changes they saw necessary. Where the school was lacking in the resources to support the changes, the parents pooled their efforts and provided the resources. Additionally, all major changes were approved by the parents before they were implemented. The parents were also very active on the school improvement committee and attended the annual staff and school development seminars so that they could inform developmental plans for the school.

SECTION 2: THE METHODOLOGY

Table 4

Types and Number of Home Support Engagements in the Categories of Parenting, Communicating and Volunteering in Each School.

Categories of home support engagements	Webly High	McDonald High	James High	Spain High
Parenting	Parenting Seminars twice annually	Parenting Seminars once annually	Parenting Seminars once annually	Parenting Seminars once annually
Communicating	A Strong PTA that meets once per term. Approximately 90% of the parents attend.	A Strong PTA that meets twice per term. Approximately 60% of the parents attend	PTA meets once per term. Approximately 30% of the parents attend.	PTA meets once per term. Approximately 30% of the parents attend.
	Annual three days academic conference and distribution of reports	Annual two days academic conference and distribution of reports	Annual two days academic conference and distribution of reports	Annual two days academic conference and distribution of reports
	Timetabled weekly parent teacher conferencing	One prizing giving ceremony per year to celebrate students success with parents	One prizing giving ceremony per year to celebrate students success with parents – usually poorly attended by parents	One prizing giving ceremony per year to celebrate students' success with parents – usually poorly attended by parents.
	Three prizing giving ceremonies per year to celebrate students success with parents			
	School text messaging system, a website, email system, PTA executive WhatsApp group, WhatsApp group by classes, social pages, school management system,	School text messaging system, a website, email system, PTA executive WhatsApp group, principal number shared with parents social pages, school management system	School text messaging system, a website, email system, WhatsApp group, principal number shared with parents social pages, school management system	School written bulletin system, PTA executive committee WhatsApp group, principal number shared with parents, school management system
	Monthly class meeting with parents conducted by Form Teachers.			
	Termly Year Group Meeting with parents led by the Year Group Supervisors			
	Principal office hours – principal is schedule 2 hours per week to see parents with or without an appointment.			

Categories of home support engagements	Webly High	McDonald High	James High	Spain High
Volunteering	Parents volunteer as managers of clubs and society, mentors, teachers, presenters at conferences, leaders of planning committees for fundraisers, teachers' day event, and welfare activities. They lead devotion exercises at the school as well. Annual orientation for new students and parents led by parents Parent treat for teachers annually	Parents volunteer as managers of clubs and society, presenters at conferences, leaders of committees like disciplinary and welfare and fundraising committees. They lead devotion exercises at the school as well.	Parents volunteer as leaders of planning committees such as welfare and fundraisers. They lead devotion exercises at the school as well.	Parents volunteer as leaders of planning committees such as welfare, fundraisers, safety and security

Table 5

Types and Number of Home Support Engagements in the Categories of Learning at Home, Decision Making and Collaborating in Each School.

Categories of home support engagements	Webly High	McDonald High	James High	Spain High
Learning at Home	Tips are shared with parents on what they can do to help their children to learn by the parent leaders, teachers and the principal. Parents are provided with the curriculum guides and the course outlines for each subject area so that they can acquaint themselves with what is being done on a weekly basis. Nothing is done deliberately to teach them the content but the parents we have seek external or additional support for their children if they are failing.	Tips are shared with parents on what they can do to help their children to learn by the principals and teachers. It is difficult to teach parents the subject content but we rather teach them how to offer guidance such as setting a study schedule, signing completed assignments etc. Just things to ensure that the work is done.	Tips are shared with parents on what they can do to help their children to learn by the principals and teachers	Tips are shared with parents on what they can do to help their children to learn by the Guidance Counselor and the Dean of Discipline.

SECTION 2: THE METHODOLOGY

Categories of home support engagements	Webly High	McDonald High	James High	Spain High
Decision Making	The president of the PTA sits on the school board and the sub committees that govern the school. The PTA leaders meet monthly with teachers to discuss policies, school rules and suggestions for improvement, they agitate for changes to food menu options and all major changes are sanctioned by them before implemented. Parents are on the school improvement committee and thus inform the plans for development.	The PTA president sits on the school board and matters are raised there for action. At each board meeting, the meeting never concludes without hearing from the pta.	The PTA president sits on the school board, which is the highest decision making body in the school. Suggestions are shared at the PTA where a majority rule carries. At each board meeting, the meeting never concludes without hearing from the PTA representative.	The PTA president sits on the school board, which is the highest decision making body in the school. Suggestions are shared at the PTA where a majority rule carries. Parents inform decision on school fees, uniform standards, rules, homework, book rental and school improvement.
Collaborating	The immediate community leaders are met with to educate them on what we are doing as a school and the kind of support we need from them in helping the students. They protect the school from vandalism and we patronize their businesses. We adopt the neighboring schools by supporting their programs through attendance and facilitate study tours from other schools. The wider community involves the past students and private sector. We are very fortunate as we get much more support because our past students are the ones leading the companies and will ensure that the school benefits where possible. We get internships and scholarships from the past students' companies. Our summer internship leads sometimes to job prospects for our students and the giving is paid forward by these students when they get older. The collaboration is amazing.	We collaborate with our community by offering them jobs in our summer repairs initiative. We use the community field in sporting activities and they use our sporting facilities as well. The community supports our fundraisers and we host an annual health fair for the community and a children treat for the neighboring infant schools. We give financial support to community led projects as well. We also collaborate with our past students association as they give funding support to many of our programs especially in the area of sports.	The school facilitates a good relationship with the community by employing community members and by soliciting their support in sporting and fundraising activities.	The school facilitates a good relationship with the community by hosting an annual community sports day, and participates in the community development committee meetings. Workers are employed from the community in school development projects and they protect the school from vandalism.

Though collaborating activities existed in all four schools, the kinds of collaborations varied. In this category, schools were found to employ members of the immediate school community and shared the use of their sporting facilities with the local communities. The schools patronized the businesses in the communities, procured the services of the community members as needed, and hosted health fairs and treats for them. The community members were found to give support to fundraising activities, such as barbeques held by the schools and helped to protect the institutions from vandalism. At Webly High, they made time to sensitize the immediate community about the school operations and the kinds of support that they needed from them to help the students, such as, reporting the children who loitered in the community during school time. They adopted the neighboring schools by supporting their programs through attendance and facilitated study tours from other schools. Webly High School also collaborated with their past students and the private sector. They obtain support from the private sector readily because their past students are the leaders or managers in several of these companies/corporations and they ensured that the school benefited where possible. In addition to providing direct funding to the school, internships and scholarships were also offered through these institutions to students. The close relationship between the school, past students, and the various organizations with which they are affiliated has provided employment opportunities for young graduates from the school. From this partnership, young graduates are expected to pay forward the benefits received in the foreseeable future. This collaboration was described as amazing by Mr. Keith James, a teacher at the school.

Barriers and Bridges Impacting Home Support Engagements

All the respondents were asked whether they were satisfied with the level of support they have given to home-support engagements in the schooling of their children. All agreed that they were not satisfied with their level of involvement in the home-support engagements and that they were desirous of doing more. The challenges that prevented them from doing more were explained as lack of time, monetary resources, and spousal support. The parents wished that they had more time to get involved but the demands of work prevented them from doing more than they currently did. Both the teachers and parents explained that they found it difficult to make themselves available to participate in after school activities after work. Day activities that were time tabled were not a problem for teachers, especially if classes were suspended to facilitate the activities, but evening demands were found to be difficult, as they were also parents and spouses, and those roles were accompanied by responsibilities that conflicted with after school demands. The parents further explicated that being a single parent made it difficult to engage in after work engagements, as a number of them have more than one child and so would have multiple school engagements to participate in but the lack of spousal or family support did not allow them to do so. They further expounded that if home-support engagements could be arranged creatively; or if the government could mandate workplaces to make allowances for workers to engage in school engagements during work hours, or if schools could use technology to support their conferences/meetings, then they would be better able to support their children's education. The principals on the other hand, saw it as their duty to put the home-support engagements in place and were willing to make themselves available for all engagements and to ensure that they work effectively.

When asked what influenced the desire to be more involved in home-support engagements, all respondents pointed to the overall proven benefits of such engagements to student and school. The principals professed that they loved to see the children excel and that student success inspires them to do more and to work harder. They believed that it was their job to make the students do well and so they tried many activities to make that happen. Some expressed that they desired to operate a good school, one that surpassed the minimum standards of the education sector and one that parents and students admired. According to the principals, the administrators cannot grow schools alone; therefore, if a greater number of parents become involved and schools did more to facilitate home-support engagements, then students and schools will perform better. Further to this, the principals outlined that when a school performs well; its reputation is linked to the school leader and influences the level of respect received by him/her from parents, teachers, and other stakeholders. This poor reputation also negatively impacts the principal's chances of getting a job at another educational institution, which may be bigger and heavily sought after. For e.g., if the principal of a small upgraded high school is known as a good principal by virtue of operating a school, which earned the ranking of good or above he/she increases his or her chances of leading a larger traditional high school, a move that may come with an increased income. Statements received from the interviews typifying the aforementioned, were as follows:

Mr. Marlie Small (pseudonym) – principal of Spain High
I am motivated to be involved because I love my students. It's a joy to see them at play, being happy at school and excelling. The reality is that, things are not the way they used to be and so, only the person that is prepared for the demands of the working world survives. I want all my students to have a fighting chance to succeed.... I want the best for them and this motivates me.

Mr. Ralph Reid (pseudonym) - principal of McDonald High
I am concerned as a principal about my reputation. I don't like it when it is said that you are the principal of a failing school. That affects me personally and my prospects to earn in the future if I so desire to move to another area in education. This motivates me to work harder to get the parents involved and to inspire the children to perform and to follow the school rules.

The parents, on other hand, outlined that they were motivated to support their children's learning because they wanted them to excel at school and to obtain a respectable job in society. They further delineated that they were aware that if they showed interest in their children, they would likely do better. It was explained by some parents that how much they did in supporting the education of their children was not only influenced by the availability of time, but how much support their children needed. Some parents explained that when their children function at a high level, their support is usually manifested in buying books and communicating high expectations and not necessarily by offering support at the school. When their children's performances fall below average, special privileges were removed to help them refocus on their learning.

For the teachers, they proffered that they were inspired to support students in doing well because it was what kept them driven to do their jobs. According to Mr. Aston Tapper a teacher on the staff of James High School, "When children do well it makes all the personal sacrifices worth it." Some of the teachers explained that the interest of parents and the interest of students influenced them as well. They were of the belief that if a parent or a student is genuinely interested in learning, they will do anything to support that student. In demonstrating support and appreciation of the expressed interests of the students and their parents, the teachers sometimes offered extra lessons without a charge or even sacrificed personal time to review work and give feedback. It must be noted also, according to Ms. Marcia Fitt (pseudonym), a teacher on the staff of Spain High School, "If your students did well, you earned the reputation of a good educator and consequently the respect of administrators and colleagues." Ms. Kerry Gayle (pseudonym), a teacher on the staff of McDonald High School, explained similarly that "I was promoted to a senior teacher because I was famous for getting all my students to pass all their external exams."

The Dynamics of Stewardship of Home-Support Engagements

When the respondents were asked about who led the home support engagements in their schools, all except the members of Webly High School, said that the engagements were led by the principals and the PTA executive members. Webly High School, which had many more activities than the other schools and had a higher support rate from parents, revealed that the engagements were led by the parents supported by the principal. As seen in Figure 4, of the 16 participants, 8 agreed that home-support engagements should be led by parents; 4 said it should be led by the school and 4 said it should be led jointly by the school and parents. It must be noted, however, that the parents and teachers of the schools rated as below average by the NEI all agreed that home-support engagements should be led by the school or jointly. Those parents were of the belief that if the principal decided on an activity, the parents would be more willing to participate, since it is the principal who is in charge and, thus, has the influence to get more done.

There were also varying views as to which activities must be led by parents, school or both. The general belief was that the school should take the lead on implementing curriculum support activities: teaching of classes, organization of parent teacher conferences, preparation of course outlines, and the development of school rules. The respondents further shared that parents should take the lead on specific activities such as fundraising, homework supervision, and students' preparation

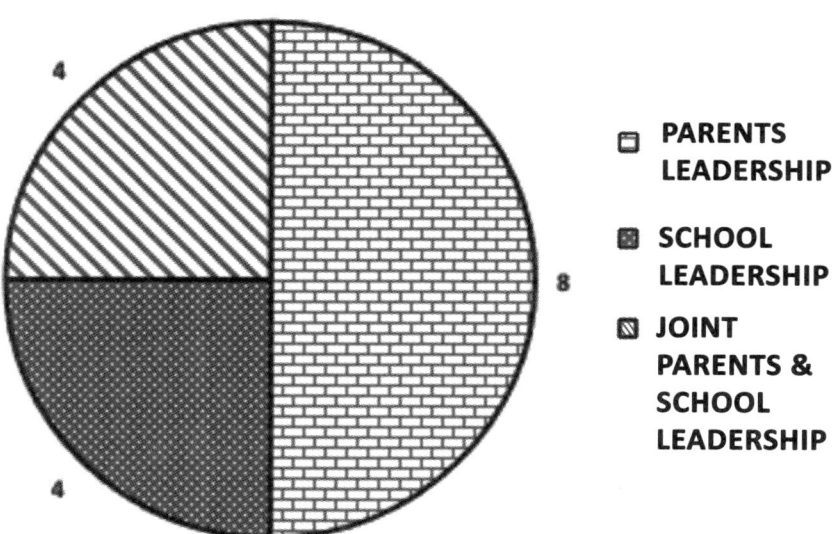

Figure 4. Respondents' views on who should lead home-support engagements.

for school and classes. As it related to jointly shared activities, it was felt that activities such as parent training seminars, support for extra-curricular activities, and school development activities should be among these.

The Accountability Dilemma

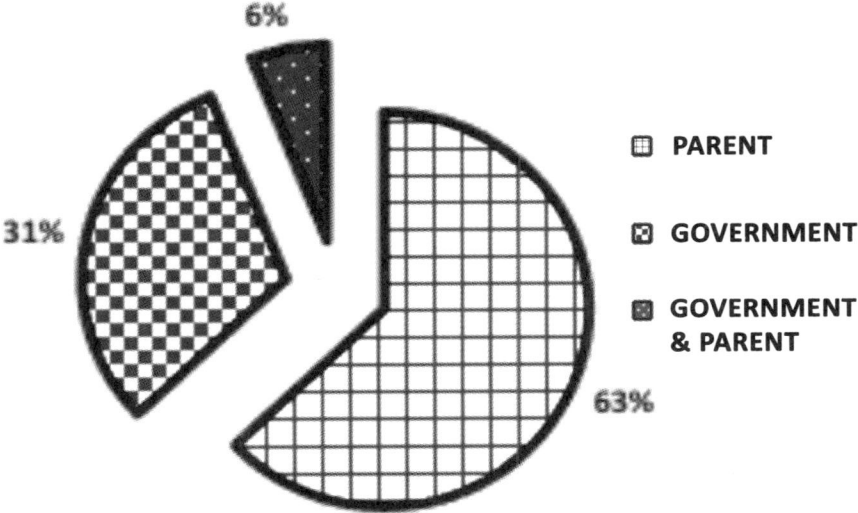

Figure 5. Stakeholders who should be held accountable for home-support engagements.

When the respondents were asked who they believed should be held responsible for home support engagements in schools, there were mixed responses. As seen in Figure 5, 63% of the respondents believed that the parents should be held accountable, 31% believed it should be the government, and 6% believed it should be both the government and the parents. It was further reiterated that if parents were made to give greater support to the schools with which they were associated, that support would help to increase academic performance. They further added that the lack of sanctions for parental noninvolvement was a contributing factor to poor student performance. It was expressed that parent support in the schooling of a child should be seen as a responsibility and that the government should put legislation in place to sanction parents for failure to support school activities as well as conduct campaigns that will build their parenting capacity. According to Mr. Ralph Reid, principal of James High School:

> I think the government has to legislate accountability issues for parents, and they must ensure that it is done. This will solve maybe 50% of the country's problem. There are students who are not given the support, but their parents are well dressed or their house well prepared but nothing or not enough support for the child's learning. Parents should be held accountable for this kind of neglect.

In an effort to provide further understanding on the accountability of stakeholders with respect to home-support engagements, the respondents were asked about the ways in which these stakeholders can be held accountable. They expounded by explaining that the government should hold parents accountable by enforcing the child rights laws of the land. According to the respondents, there are laws that speak to neglect of duty and consequences for other forms of child abuse, but the government has not enforced these laws consistently. They posited that the schools should be made to report on the level of support students received with respect to schooling and the government should take action in the best interest of the children, whether by helping the parents financially or providing parenting support. In addition to application of government sanctions, it was proposed by the respondents that children should respectfully encourage their parents to give support in schooling engagements by communicating how important it is to them when their parents showed interest in their learning. Ms. Kerry Gayle a teacher on the staff of McDonald High School stated:

> When the parents do not prepare students for school and fail to supervise their homework, this is neglect of duty. The

schools should be asked to provide a report on this monthly and the state should take action against parents in the best interest of the children. The state can give more benefits to students such as books, grants, and so on, if the parents do their part in the schooling of their child. So they can give the subsidy if the parents attend meetings, volunteer at the school among other things as agreed as important by the government and the schools. A points plan could be developed and used to motivate the parents to do their part.

Some respondents further expressed that the school had a role to play in holding parents accountable and that the government should mandate that schools implement motivational activities and training sessions to encourage home-support engagements and enable parents to take more responsibility for home support. Some of the respondents also believed that schools should engender a reporting and reward system for parental involvement as a way to hold parents more accountable. If parents are not attending school conferences, meetings, or supervising homework activities, this information should be captured and reported to the government. The information should then be used to inform intervention programs to ensure accountability. It was further explained that where schools had not established activities to get parents involved, this information should be used to influence the rank of that schools, which has implications for the reputation of the schools. Some respondents believed that this would be effective in encouraging home-support engagements in schools.

When the respondents were asked whether the ranking of a school by the NEI should be influenced by the quality or quantity of home-support engagements, approximately 88% of the respondents said no to this question. It was further explained that too many of the schools were struggling to obtain the participation of the majority of the parents and if the quality and quantity of home-support engagements were used to rank schools, too many schools would be deemed failing, despite their efforts. Such an approach, if taken, could result in demotivated school staff and students with low morale and low school spirit. It was felt by all the educators that though they do not want parent support to be a criterion for ranking schools, it was being indirectly used, because most of the schools that ended up with a failing grade, lacked home support for school-related activities. However, 12% of the respondents were of the view that most parents want their children to be in a good school and if they knew that their lack of support was negatively impacting the reputation of the schools, they would be more inclined to become more involved.

Insights from the Findings

An examination of the discourse with the respondents of this study revealed several insights that were reflective of the home-school-community partnership model proposed by Epstein (2001). The model posited 6 categories of parent involvement and defined home-support engagement as "parents working together with the school to create school-like opportunities, events, and programs that reinforce, recognize, and reward students for good progress, creativity, contributions, and excellence" (Epstein, 1995, p. 702). It is synonymous with the term parent involvement and included all the activities in which parents might engage at home and at school in support of their children's learning and academic success, activities planned either by school personnel or parents or both (Epstein, 1995, 2011; Fantuzzo, Tighe, & Childs, 2000).

It was found from the data that parents of high performing schools with high performing children were more aware of the performance of the schools they were associated with and knew how high and low performance were defined in their schools. The data showed that the level of support for home-support engagements was highest in the schools rated as good by the NEI across all stakeholder groups.

According to Epstein (2005), home-school partnerships were organized within 6 categories of involvement and there were 2 kinds of interactions within the categories, around which the engagements were operationalized: standard and general interactions. The standard interactions were those organizational interactions between families and schools, such as communication between home and school in the form of reports and correspondences about school activities and performance.

The specific interactions were those between teachers and parents: the sending of notes or direct communication, which took place at a parent teachers' conference (Epstein, 2005). Therefore, the fact that the awareness of the parents of the high performing schools and children was higher could suggest that these schools have more operable standards and specific interactions that kept the parents abreast of the schools' happenings as seen in Tables 4 and 5. It could also mean that the parents were more involved by their own volition and interest or the barriers to their involvement were bridged by the myriad of interactions in those schools. The converse could also be drawn about schools that were ranked below good by the NEI and were assigned students with low scores; they had less standard and specific interactions that created further barriers to home support and, thus, had a body of parents who lacked the knowledge on the school performance standards and rankings. This could mean that the more opportunities there are for interactions, be it standard or specific, the greater the likelihood that parents would be aware of school standards and be engaged in more home-support engagements.

Shared Meanings of Home Support Engagements

The respondents in this study, despite using varied terminologies, provided similar definitions of home support engagements. These definitions were mainly characterized by their experiences (what they did for students/children) as well as an overarching philosophy that informed what they engaged in. The principals and teachers described home-support engagements similarly, as all stakeholders working together to support the student's success in school. This construction of home-support engagement showed consideration for all stakeholders, the parents, school, community, and the government. This definition of home support engagement has implications for the persons from whom support may be solicited to foster an effective home-school partnership. It must be noted also, that though the parents saw it as efforts to ensure students success in school, they spoke mostly of home support engagement from an emotional stand point. They saw it as the demonstration of love and encouragement that parents gave to their children to ensure they did well as students. According to the parent respondents, it involved the participating in school activities such as meetings, fundraising, and buying school supplies to show how much they cared about their children and their learning.

Shared Value for Home-Support Engagements

All the respondents agreed that home-support engagement was very important as it ensured students success and by extension the success that the schools would have in producing rounded students such as a successful reputation and alumni who could give back to the development of the school. They further unanimously declared that though all stakeholders benefitted from home-support engagements, it was the students who benefitted the most and strongly reiterated that no one stakeholder could do it alone but rather through a partnership. This was consistent with Epstein (2001) who posited that home support engagements benefitted everyone as students' learning improved, schools improved, teachers were assisted, and families were strengthened. Further to this, though the terminologies were different, a common denominator of the findings revealed that both parents and educators recognized that there was a role for each stakeholder in educating a child, that the roles were similar across stakeholder groups, and focused on ensuring the success of the child (Epstein, 2001). This shared interest was clearly influenced by the beliefs, attitudes, and values of the stakeholders (Epstein, 2005).

Varied Stewards and Number of Home-Support Engagements in Schools

With the benefit of increasing parental participation in education, Epstein (2001) positioned a model that recognized 6 categories of educational involvement that schools could use to engage parents and the wider community, the organization of which provided a framework for schools that hoped to increase family school interactions. All these proposed categories of home-support engagements were present in all 4 schools but the number of activities and the level of support given were higher in some schools than others, as well as the fact that the lead organizers of the engagements varied across schools. This was likely as it was only by working together and engaging in the 6 categories of educational involvement, that stakeholders were able to create the partnerships that supported short term and long-term student success (Epstein, 2005).

Therefore, what pertained in a school was a reflection of the level of partnership that existed between stakeholders and the level success that they might attain. For e.g., in the schools that were rated as good by the NEI, home-support engagements were seen to be higher (see Tables 4 and 5), educators and parents were aware of the ranking of the schools by the NEI, and how quality student performance was defined. The types of involvement activities were much higher in numbers and the lead implementers of the activities were principals and parents. All the schools were found to have a PTA, however, the difference in terms of the parents' support at the PTA meetings ranged from a low of 30% to 90% with the schools rated as good boasting the higher percentage support. Whilst the parents in the schools ranked as good could fluently share on the activities that took place in their schools, the parents of the low-ranking schools struggled to articulate same.

According to Epstein (2005), the interactions within and between the family and school were the most important in a child's education, be it the standard or specific interactions. In addition to the fact that all categories of involvement were found to be present in the 4 schools, it was also found that all the interactions within the schools could also be classified under a category of involvement as proposed by Epstein (2001). However, 4 of the categories were found to be pervasive in all 4 schools: communicating, decision making, parenting and volunteering. The category of learning at home was found to have the least number of engagements in all 4 schools. This was indicative of how home support was being practiced, the importance of these activities to the stakeholders, the needs that they served, as well as the overarching philosophy governing what was implemented in a bid to enable home support.

The activities under each of these categories were also found to be school led and thus were suggestive of who was leading the implementation of home-support engagements in the education process. Though there were mixed responses as to who should lead home support engagements, most of the respondents expressed that they believed it should be led by parents. However, from a review of the engagements that were being executed in each school, it was clear that those that were school led were more frequent, sustained, and the general perception was that principals and parents gave the most support. This perception could be fostered due to the number of standard interactions as against specific interactions in each category of activities. The data showed that in each school, the home-support engagements were largely standard interactions and not specific interactions which were mainly teacher led (Epstein, 2001). Therefore, the more the engagements were focused on the standard interactions; it could mean that the teachers might continue to be perceived as giving the least support for home-support engagements. Consequently, efforts might be necessary to incorporate the teachers in the standard interactions to reflect a greater partnership on their part. The fact that the greatest support was perceived to be given by the principals was also instructive, as principal support has been found to greatly influence the quality of partnership programs (Epstein, 2001). It must be noted however, that in the school that had the greatest level of parent support, leadership of the home-support engagements was delivered by the parents. This could suggest that the more engagements that were implemented in a school, the more opportunities might be available for parents to lead and partner for students' success.

Home Support Catalysts

Under the category of parenting, the home support engagement was focused predominantly on training in parenting skills for all 4 schools. It must be noted that this was enabled by a national focus on parenting in the month of November. This insinuates that national support of this nature could be helpful in shaping home support for students learning and reiterated the finding of Epstein (2005) that stated that shared interests and influences could be promoted by the policies, actions, beliefs, attitudes and values of the stakeholders. A national policy could therefore enable more involvement in support of realizing the mutual interest of students' success. Also, the schools that had higher numbers of engagements were those with higher parent involvement. According to Epstein (2001), shared involvement was not limited by number, but rather could be increased with concerted effort by one or more of the stakeholders. This might mean that the more parents were involved, the more opportunities were created for increased engagements and ultimately improvement in students' outcomes.

According to Epstein (2001), time and experience were two factors that influenced the degree of involvement by each stakeholder group. Epstein further posited that though parents were found to be more involved in school when their children were young, involvement was also influenced by the ability of the child and by extension, the culture and reputation of the school. In this study, it was found that all the principals and teachers were knowledgeable of the ranking of their schools by the NEI as well as the descriptions of high and low performance in their schools. Though there was no notable gender difference in the awareness levels of the respondents, the parents of the schools ranked good were aware of the ranking and the descriptions of high and low performance in their schools while the parents of the unsatisfactory and below schools were unaware of the ranking of the school and were unsure of the descriptions of high and low performance in the schools that they were affiliated with.

This was indicative of the position that the ability of the child and by extension, the culture and reputation of the school could impact the quality and quantity of involvement of the stakeholder groups. The parents of the higher performing students were more aware and involved, and the school with the culture of involvement had parents who were more aware. Consequently, how the child and the school have performed could influence the degree to which schools, families, and communities partnered to ensure the child's success (Epstein, 2001).

In respect to the motivations for involvement in home-support engagements, all the respondents explained that their greatest motivation was the proven benefits of home-support engagements to the students' success as well as that of the school. Additionally, the principals were also motivated by the sense of duty they felt in ensuring that a home-school partnership existed in their schools. It was felt by all principals that it was their job to engage parents in the education process. Other motivational factors included the benefits of improved professional reputation of the school leaders/teachers, the opportunity for promotion, the interests of the students and their parents, and the students increased opportunities to obtain respectable jobs in society that was very important to the parents. The parents were also motivated by the abilities of their children. Some parents explained that if their children had the ability and were functioning at a high level, they tended to do less at the school but do more like buying their books and communicating high expectations for them. Where their children fell below average in their performance, some parents tended to remove special privileges. Based on these factors, it was evident that home and school activities were not separate but sequential; both the school and the home were driven by similar and varied factors and played leading roles at different periods in the child's life (Epstein, 2001).

Another notable influencing factor of home support was the ideology of who should be leading the interactions. While most persons believed that it should be led by parents, it must be noted that parents of the underperforming students and school felt it should be led by the school. This could mean that if the school failed to engage parents, the parents might also fail to get involved. This was instructive therefore to the design and implementation of the home-support partnership especially in underperforming schools. The general belief however, was that the school should take the implementing lead on curriculum support activities, such as: teaching of classes, organization of parent teacher conferences, preparation of course outlines and the development of school rules, and parents should take the lead on specific activities such as fundraising, homework supervision, and students preparation for school and classes. As it related to jointly shared activities, it was felt that activities such as parent training seminars, support for extracurricular activities, and school development activities should be among these.

Redefining Methods of Home-Support Engagements

Though motivated by varied and shared reasons, all respondents expressed that they were not satisfied with their level of involvement in the home-support engagements in the schooling of the children in their care and that they were desirous of doing more. While the principals saw their involvement as a sense of duty that propelled their inputs, the challenges that prevented the stakeholders from getting more involved were explained to be the lack of time, monetary resources, and spousal support. This presented insights into how home-support engagements could be organized for greater effectiveness. The respondents bemoaned the need for state support, use of technology, and a redefinition of how support was measured and implemented as means of increased parent involvement. The school and home therefore need to be aware of the challenges each faced in ensuring the success of students and work to overcome these challenges to successfully engage all stakeholders in a successful home-school partnership (Epstein, 2001). Epstein et al. (2002) also opined that a redefinition of the traditional interactions was needed for greater diversity and inclusivity in home and school partnerships.

The belief an individual holds about a phenomenon may influence their actions towards it. Hence if it was the belief of some parents that the school was the leader of home-support engagements, then they might resolve to do less than they could do. This could also mean that for changes to occur in this regard, one might have to reorient the stakeholders to a new way of thinking as the leadership of a school involves all stakeholders while the implementation of policies and activities might be led by varied persons. As a consequence, there might need to be clarity between leadership and implementation of an agreed policy among stakeholders.

Instructive also to the design of home-support partnerships was the expressed belief that there should be a minimum standard of activities that all stakeholders should engender to foster and that there was a general preference for some categories of engagements. The minimum home-support engagements for all schools were strongest in the categories of communicating, parenting, volunteering, and decision making. The specific ones that were shared were: an active PTA with at least 70% of the parents attending, parent consultation time to discuss students' performance, parent involvement through volunteerism in extracurricular activities and fundraising, systems to ensure homework was done, parenting skills sessions, decision making avenues regarding school programs, and two-way communication opportunities. The engagements that were proposed to be nonnegotiable were attendance to PTA meetings and the parent consultation meetings where students' performance could be discussed. It was further suggested that each parent must attend at least one of these activities annually. Other minimum level activities were suggested such as parents volunteering to lead extracurricular activities, systems to ensure students' homework was completed, and students were prepared for school. The dominant category of home support engagement as a minimum standard for parents focused mainly on the category of communicating.

It was believed however, that in order to improve home support, improvements needed to be made in the parenting category of involvement. It was suggested that efforts should be exerted in the areas of parenting skills. It was the belief of the respondents that if parents could be trained into how to demonstrate love for their children, valuing their children and how to be an effective parent, then they might get more involved in home-support engagements. It was also articulated that if schools could be given more time and resources to do home visits then parents and children could be more supported. Some of the respondents also suggested an incentive scheme to motivate home-support engagements. In expounding on this, it was explained that home and schools could work out a points system for each agreed home-support engagement that existed in their school and parents could be allowed to earn points and rewarded with medals or scholarships for their children based on how many points they earned. It was further said that a special grant could be given to schools that implemented parental involvement activities by the government as a way of improving home-support engagements.

Accountability for Home Support Engagements

Though it was the view that principals have given the most support and that they were the ones leading the engagements, it was strongly felt that it was the parents (63%) followed by the government (31%) that should be held accountable for home-support engagements in schools. As it related to how effectively this could be done, it was explained that the government should hold parents accountable by enforcing the child rights laws of the land. According to the respondents, there were laws that spoke to neglect of duty and consequences of other forms of child abuse but the government does not enforce these laws consistently. They posited that the schools should be made to report on the level of support students received with respect to schooling and the government should take action in the best interest of the children, whether by helping the parents financially, or providing other forms of parent support.

Some respondents further expressed that the school had a role in holding the parents accountable and that the government should mandate the schools to implement motivational activities and training sessions to encourage home support engagements and make parents more accountable. Some of the respondents also believed that schools should engender a reporting and reward system for parental involvement as a way to help parents to be more accountable. If parents were not attending school conferences, meetings, or supervising homework activities, a resource could be in the school to capture this data and to report it to the government. The government could then use this data to inform the types of intervention that would be made available to increased parental accountability. It was further explained that where schools lacked the established activities to get parents involved, this could be used to rank the schools. The rank of a school tended to influence its reputation and its ability to attract high performing students. If school personnel knew this, then greater efforts might be exerted in the implementation of home-support engagements in their schools.

Approximately 88% of the respondents said the ranking of a school by the NEI should not be influenced by the quality or quantity of home-support engagements. It was further explained that too many of the schools were struggling to obtain the participation of the majority of the parents in the schooling of their children and if that was used to rank schools, too many of the schools would be failing despite the efforts of school leaders and teachers. This might unfairly result in demotivated school staff and students, producing low morale and low school spirit that would only make the situation worse. Ironically, it was felt by all the educators that this indirectly influenced the rankings of the NEI as most of the schools that ended up with a failing grade were schools that tended to lack home support for school-related activities. However, 12% of the respondents were of the view that most parents wanted their children to be in a good school and if they knew that their lack of support was negatively impacting the reputation of their school, they might be inclined to be more involved.

SUMMARY

The key finding of the study was that all the stakeholders in a child's education had mutual interests and influences. The primary shared interest was a caring concern that each child be provided with the opportunity to become successful (see Epstein, 2001). Additionally, the findings suggested that stakeholders' shared interests and influences could be promoted by several motivational factors, be it policies, beliefs, benefits, leadership, personal challenges, available resources, enabling strategies, attitudes, and/or values of the stakeholders. By working together and engaging in the 6 categories of educational involvement, stakeholders can help to create partnerships that could support short-term and long-term student success. However, all partners must be aware of the motivational factors that might facilitate these partnerships, the barriers that might hinder them and even the proposed implementation of the minimum standards of involvement, and an accountability framework that could assist in overcoming these barriers. All of these are instrumental in support of the success of the child who must remain in the center of the interactions throughout the education process and thus these were incorporated into the development of an incentivized home support program detailed in the following section.

Section 3:
The Project

INTRODUCTION

The results of this study have shown that all the interviewed stakeholders had shared interests and influences in the educational journey of the children in their charge. The primary mutual interest was that each child should be afforded the opportunity to become successful. The data suggested that stakeholders' shared interests and influences could be promoted by several motivational factors: policies, beliefs, benefits, leadership, personal challenges, available resources, enabling strategies, attitudes, and/or the values of the stakeholders. Therefore, by working together through engagement in the 6 categories of educational involvement as posited by Epstein (2001), establishing a minimum standard of involvement that reflects the motivations of parents, mitigating the challenges that thwart parent involvement, incorporating parent leadership, and leveraging government support, home support engagements can be increased and sustained.

From these findings, a training manual or a professional development program on parent involvement in education could be derived; however, these are many and would not add much value to this field of study. Based on the findings from this study and the local education context, it was found to be more valuable to incorporate the information gleaned from this research in the development of a comprehensive incentivized school funding policy, which would seek to address the need for increased parental involvement through an inclusive home support program, thereby, leading to increased student success. The data showed that there were gaps in the home-school engagement standards and structures both at the national and local levels of the education system in Jamaica which could be creatively responded to by a policy framework with its attendant procedures.

In light of the above, the outcome for this case study was a policy recommendation that outlined the position taken on the issue of home-school engagement as informed by the findings of this study and the rationale for that position in an effort to generate support for its diffusion. Therefore, the ensuing policy recommendation provides the evidence to support the need for the proposed framework that could be used to redefine and incentivize home support engagements to facilitate efforts at improved student performance in the Jamaican education system. Authoritative references to validate the position, an exploration of the strengths and weaknesses of the position, as well as possible solutions or courses of action are encapsulated in this policy recommendation.

Policy Background

The current educational reform process in Jamaica continues to echo the need for the delivery of quality education and equity for all students (Ministry of Education, Youth and Information, 2017). In an effort to achieve this, the government through the Ministry of Education, Youth and Information has implemented several strategies to improve school leadership, curriculum offerings, school monitoring and school funding. The implementation of these strategies has resulted in the establishment of an educational leadership college,

SECTION 3: THE PROJECT

named the National College for Educational Leadership which is an agency established under the Jamaica Education System Transformation Program with the directive to ensure that there is equity and quality in leadership at the infant up to the tertiary levels of the education system through training and support of all school leaders (National College for Educational Leadership, 2017). The NEI (2014), another of the strategic decisions of the government, was established to ensure that schools are frequently assessed and guided towards operations above the minimum standards for learning institutions. In 2016, the government commenced the implementation of the National Standard Curriculum designed to ensure that all students are exposed to high quality standard of learning for their optimal development (Angus, 2016). In its bid to achieve equity and quality, the government has also embarked on the introduction of a new funding policy for the secondary level schools which resulted in each high school receiving an increase from JD$11,500.00 to a maximum of JD$19,000.00 per student enrolled in each high school (Ministry of Education, Youth and Information, 2017).

These strategic activities of the government of Jamaica are intended to have a positive impact on the education system. However, this intended impact could be strengthened with increased support from the homes and families of the children that the system serves, as better value for educational investment is guaranteed when home and school work together constructively (Santana, Rothstein, & Bain, 2016). According to Baek and Bullock (2015), if the school, family and state collaborate, this reduces the debilitating factors and enhances the factors that guarantee that students maximize their potential. The need to influence the involvement of parents in the education process is, therefore, central to the quest for improved students' performance or to address the achievement gap. A plan for permanent funding for parental involvement is a positive step towards an effective parent engagement program (Baek & Bullock, 2015) as well as the thrust for equity and quality education for all students.

An in-depth examination of the educational funding policy of the Jamaican government showed that the amount of money that is allocated to each student in each school is arrived at using a suite of premiums (Ministry of Education, Youth and Information, 2017). In the secondary schools in Jamaica, for example, a JD$19,000.00 maximum is given per year for each student to be educated and this sum is arrived at accordingly: JD$11,500 for tuition, JD $2,000 for curriculum support, JD$2,000 for students pursuing technical and vocational subjects, JD $1,500 for maintenance, and JD $2,000 for students who are beneficiaries of the government's welfare program (Ministry of Education, Youth and Information, 2017). Additionally, parents are given the option to make a non-mandatory contribution to the program of education by paying a sum of money as agreed by the parent body and ratified by the school board (Ministry of Education, Youth and Information, 2017). An analogous concept could be used to accomplish greater equity and quality in the education system through in the incentivization of parent involvement, in that, students could be granted additional funding support for educational endeavors based on the involvement of schools and parents in the established home-school engagements within a school. In so doing, a home-school support premium could be included in the funding policy of the government, which could encourage schools to include focused parental activities in their program of education or school improvement plans, leverage more interest and support from parents, thereby, creating the potential for increased opportunities for students to improve in their learning.

REVIEW OF LITERATURE

The groundwork in relation to home-school engagement is clearly advanced as there is congruence among policymakers that a critical component of any mandate to improve students' outcomes is for educators to improve family-school relations and increase parental involvement in education (McWilliam, 2015). The evidence of this stance was strongly underscored in the 2002 reauthorization of the Elementary and Secondary Education Act (ESEA), better known as the No Child Left Behind Act (U.S. Department of Education, n.d.), which mandated that states seeking funding for Title I – low income schools – should identify and implement practices for involving parents that are "based on the most current research that meets the highest professional and technical standards, on effective parental involvement that fosters achievement to high standards for all children" (Section 1111.d). The 2015 reauthorization, known as the Every Student Succeeds Act, maintains this commitment to parent and family engagement activities (U.S. Department of Education, n.d.). Hence, the effect of parental involvement on student achievement is of continuing interest to practitioners and policymakers alike. Like the United States, the Nigerian National Policy on Education (Federal Republic of Nigeria, 2004) included a mandate that required that local people, particularly parents, be encouraged to participate in school management. The thrust of policy development echoes the importance of home-school partnerships, and therefore, champions the call for parental involvement to be seen as a dynamic avenue that can bring about change, not only in schools and education systems, but also in homes and societies (Olibie, 2014).

According to Olibie (2014), the impetus to involve parents in education should continue, as schools should want to better their environment and performance, thereby providing the support needed for children to grow up to become productive and responsible members of society. Schools on their own cannot successfully achieve this mandate, and thus, extra school interventions are required. Funding of parental involvement programs is increasing in many countries (Merkel-Holguin, 2003) because it is recognized by practitioners as a helpful device to work with families on child protection. At the same time, asking teachers and school principals to be in charge of home engagement initiatives does not seem to be a viable approach, as the pressure on the school system is already high and teachers' overload is already a relevant issue (Argentin & Barbetta, 2016). Therefore, extra school interventions through the incentivization of home support seem to be a promising option.

Collaboration between families and schools is extremely important for the success of students as the lack of such can affect the manner in which parents and school personnel interact and participate in the schooling process (Vega, Moore III, & Miranda, 2015). In fact, when school staff and family members recognized sources of school-related support, they were more likely to tap into these sources and support their students (Hilgendorf, 2012). However, schools have yet to fully embrace the concept of active parental involvement, particularly in academic matters, and have yet to design formalized programs that provide avenues for parental involvement (Kurtulmus, 2016). A focus on the traditional approach to parental involvement neglects the inclusion of contemporary measures that are context specific or culturally responsive. As shown in this study, parents were desirous of being involved in the educational activities of their children, but this was thwarted by obstacles to direct involvement: work demands, lack of spousal support and financial challenges.

Instead of a focus on transactional models of involvement that emphasize volunteerism and homework, a collaborative design model is encouraged. More genuine and authentic forms of engagements have the potential to not only transform schools but also the community that it serves. According to Winston and Evans (2014), compensating schools for parental engagement posits a transformative potential as a starting point for more meaningful and authentic educational policy dialogues.

SECTION 3: THE PROJECT

Redefining Home School Engagement

Epstein (2001) proposed 6 categories of parental involvement. While these categories have been pervasive in home and school engagement for student development, there is need to revisit the types of activities that one could consider to be reflective of parental involvement as well as those that reflect the changing times. According to Goodall (2012), parental engagement is never complete, as each new academic year brings new cohorts of parents and children with new interests and levels of technological advancements, which require educational stakeholders to adapt to new ways of being. Many parents find engagement with schools difficult, but still have a strong desire to be involved in their children's learning and education (Cooper, 2009). However, a lack of consideration for the needs of families, such as scheduling of meetings and other activities, may remain significant barriers to active engagement of some parents (Goodall & Montgomery, 2014). Such situations could be remedied through a redefinition of home support activities through the incorporation of technology and the changing needs of parents and students. This represents a fluid model, rather than an absolute solution, as one size does not fit all.

The reality is that not all educational stakeholders are the same, have the same needs, face the same barriers, or share the same conceptualization of home school engagements (Goodall & Montgomery, 2014). A broadened understanding of parental engagement to include a diversified means or tools of engagement could lay the foundation for schools to offer appropriate support to all parents to better support their children (Goodall & Montgomery, 2014). In so doing, all stakeholders within an education setting should be encouraged and shown how to devise nontraditional ways to redefine home-support engagement to motivate parents to become involved and, thereby, conveying an inclusive method of home-support partnership, which reflects the changing times (Young, Austin, & Growe, 2013). One such way to achieve this is through the use of technology.

The rapid advancement of technology has seen people from all walks of life embracing its use and impact, and exploring its present and future potential (Pasco, 2013). Many technology inventions have helped people to connect to the world or better accomplish what they do. Some of these include: computers, mobile phones, virtual reality technology, learning management systems, texting, instant messaging, blog, tweets, multimedia, games and applications, tele/videoconferencing, emails, Skype, Zoom, and other social media. The utilization of these tools can redefine how home support engagements are designed, thereby, enabling others who might be challenged by traditional approaches. In so doing, parent conferences can be held online via Zoom, Skype or videoconferencing applications. Parenting seminars can be done using the virtual learning: synchronously or asynchronously. Parents can be invited to observe their children in a class using cameras as well as provide feedbacks using online methods of communication. The reality is that technology has opened up a world of opportunities that need to be used to the advantage of student development..

INCENTIVIZATION OF HOME SUPPORT ENGAGEMENTS

The many theories of compensation, such as reinforcement, expectancy, efficiency wage, agency, among others, have been repeatedly echoed through the presentation of evidence that incentives and reinforcement can be key drivers of important workplace behaviors or other such targeted behaviors (Gerhart & Fang, 2014). On the contrary, arguments have also been posited that providing incentives for performance or targeted behaviors can have negative results, as tangible incentives may harm intrinsic interest/motivation in work (Kohn, 1993); it may harm cooperation and teamwork where work is interdependent (Adams, 1963); and it does not fit with many national cultures and often requires adaptation (Hofstede, 1983). In spite of the criticisms, Shaw and Gupta (2015) have found that financial incentives are effective in that they can improve performance quantity and quality and may not negate the value of intrinsic motivation, but rather may maximize its effects on behaviors. They further postulated that rather than debating whether incentives work, one should instead focus on how and why they work (the conditions that enable them to work and the people they impact the most), and use this knowledge to improve targeted behaviors.

The tendency for persons to accept incentives when they are offered has been found to be varied and, in most cases, the level of acceptance by each individual is dependent on the type of behavior change that an incentive is to achieve (Whelan et al., 2014). Consequently, changing degrees of success have been achieved with the use of financial incentives to encourage a wide range of behaviors, such as uptake of childhood vaccinations in developing countries, smoking cessation, as well as uptake of antiretroviral drugs for those living with HIV (Giles, McColl, Sniehotta, & Adams, 2014). Though some researchers view the provision of financial incentives to encourage particular behaviors as divisive or coercive on the social strata (Parke, Ashcroft, Brown, Marteau, & Seale, 2013), they are convinced that other interventions are not as effective, and that the incentives to be used are effective and affordable (Giles et al., 2015). In this regard, some are of the view that incentivized programs can be acceptable, once persons understand the seriousness of the problem it intends to solve. It was also found that people are willing to trade off their dislikes of incentive programs once they are convinced of the effectiveness of the gains in intervention programs (Parke et al., 2013).

Greene et al. (2017) explored the acceptability of financial incentives among actual recipients and implementers to determine its feasibility and effectiveness in health behavior change. Their findings revealed that all the respondents, though some were skeptical in the beginning, found the financial incentives intervention programs highly acceptable. In this regard, the findings detailed 5 important factors that should be taken into consideration to obtain greater acceptance: emotional benefits, financial benefits, health related benefits, philosophical concerns, and implementation issues. Accordingly, the program should attempt to help people feel cared for and appreciated, rather than coerced; the incentives should be useful to the recipients and adherence to the plan should result in obvious improved health or behavior. Also, the implementation of the program will result in a demand for staff time and space for the disbursement of incentives, storage and tracking of gains, which may be seen as increased administrative burden. Therefore, implementation should allow for a flexible integration into regular workflow, rather than a burdensome activity. There are others who believe that a person's behavior should be self motivated, rather than externally driven, and so may feel conflicted when given an incentive for doing what they think is their responsibility to do. In such cases, persons should be allowed to decide whether or not to take the incentives or the incentives could be designed in such a way that it is only offered to those who might need it.

In both the public and private sectors, incentive pay has been found to increase worker effort, output and other desirable outcomes (Goodman & Turner, 2013). An increasing number of studies have also shown that incentives can positively improve students' behaviors; however, it remains unclear whether use of incentives can improve educational inputs related to parents (Martorell, Miller, Santibañez, & Augustine, 2016). An examination of this uncertainty found that a combination of student incentives with financial incentives for parents improved the daily attendance of students to summer school by 9% and increased the likelihood of having perfect attendance by more than 60% (Martorell et al., 2016; Ross, 2016). This finding was similar to that found by Dee (2011), who investigated the impact of parental incentives on student attendance and found that attendance increased by 5.2% when parental welfare payments were made conditional on their children's attendance to school (p. 22). Similarly, Fryer, Levitt, and List (2015) offered parents large financial incentives for participation in school-related activities, such as attendance at meetings, for completing assignments with their child at home, their child's performance on developmental assessments, and found that attendance among program parents increased to approximately 60%. Fryer et al., also provided attendance incentives to a group of parents and found that it had a large impact on parent engagement in parent education programs. They also found that a sizable portion of parents may not always engage in a program without incentives but may be more willing to become more fully engaged with incentives.

Incentives and parent programming could leverage greater home-school partnerships, as when offered together, they might help elicit desired home-school engagement behaviors, parents could learn skills to support their children's education and possibly inspire closer family ties and commitment to duty of care. Some critics might see this as an act of paying parents to do their jobs. But when done well, incentivizing home-school engagements is way more than just bribing parents with gift cards or other tangibles; it is enabling students to increase their educational outcomes and life chances.

POLICY DESCRIPTION

This policy recommendation outlines a proposed incentivized home-support engagement program, which incorporates contemporary tools to foster greater home-support engagements. It includes the 6 categories of engagements: parenting, communicating, volunteering, learning at home, decision making and collaborating, as proposed by Epstein (2001). It also includes suggested activities under each category, inclusive of the minimum number of activities that the research respondent proposed should be in all schools. The policy has 3 components: school-based, home-based and a school home-based component. The school-based component constitutes the design and execution of the home support minimum standard tier of activities as supported by the findings of this research. These include the 4 common categories of engagements (communicating, parenting, volunteering and decision making) and the activities as posited by the research participants: an active PTA with at least 70% of the parents attending, parent consultation time to discuss students' performance, facility to support parent involvement through volunteerism in extracurricular activities and fundraising, systems to ensure homework is done, parenting skills sessions, decision making avenues for parents regarding school programs, and two-way communication opportunities (p. 83). Where a school provides the evidence of these activities, the policy advocates that the government provides additional funding support to sustain these activities through the provision of a parent engagement premium at a per student ratio. This would be analogous to that of the current funding approach used by the government of Jamaica to fund secondary education, where additional funding has been provided for curriculum support using a curriculum support premium per student (JD$2,000 per student). A similar JD$2,000 could be given per student to support the school-based activities.

In the home-based component, parents could earn points for each activity that they engaged in to support the success of their children as students. The school and home would work together and establish a menu of activities in which parents may engage to enable their children's success, each of which could equate to an agreed number of points. The accumulated points would be redeemed for tangible incentives as agreed by the school and home and funded by the school, PTA and the government. A sample of this initiative is outlined in Tables 6 and 7.

In the school-home component, the school and family benefit from incentives for combination of points earned. In so doing, the number of points earned by a class or a year group is tallied and the class or group with the highest number of points earns an award for the class or year group inclusive of the affected families. Additionally, the school that earns the highest points overall, will earn an award. Table 6 shows an outline of this component.

Table 6

School-Home Incentive Program

TOTAL POINTS EARNED	INCENTIVES
Class with the highest points combined	Funded class project, class family social
Year group with the highest points combined	Funded year group project, group family social
School with the highest points combined	Funded school project, parent engagement award, school family social

In order to determine the types of incentives to which the accumulated points could be equivalent, an incentive guide has been developed and outlined in Table 7. Table 7 includes the award of grants, vouchers, tickets, gifts, among other tokens resulting from points achieved by engagement in several activities. For example, a parent who attended a PTA meeting, ensured the completion of his/her child's homework by being a signatory to it, gave resources towards school development activities, and served as a volunteer in a club or a society, could accumulate a total of 70 points and would be eligible for any token equivalent to a range of 50-100 points, for e.g., a meal voucher or a swimming pass.

POLICY IMPLEMENTATION

This policy is designed to be implemented annually during the academic school year – September to July. The implementation team for each school will include the leadership of the school, leadership of the PTA, and the Ministry of Education official/designate. It will also require the services of a data entry clerk or clerks, depending on the size of the school population. The clerk(s) will be responsible for the collation of data, the distribution of incentives and reporting on the policy initiatives. The leadership of the school, leadership of the PTA, and the Ministry of Education official/designate will consult with the members of the wider stakeholder body and agree on the school-based, home-based and school home-based tenets which will form the home-support program that the school will operate. This could reflect the program as described in the policy description above or reflect other activities according to school size, location and other contextual variables. The consultation could be guided accordingly:

SECTION 3: THE PROJECT

Implementation Plan - Stage 1: Consultation

Table 7

Incentive Chart

Sample Incentives	Proposed Value of Incentives	Sample Incentives	Proposed Value of Incentives
One day meal voucher	50 - 100 points	Book vouchers	500 - 900 points
One week meal voucher/transport vouchers	150 - 300 points	Uniform vouchers	400 - 600 points
Raffle tickets	150 - 250 points	Tertiary studies grant	5000 points and over
Barbeque tickets	150 - 250 points	Computer voucher	500 - 700 points
50% discount on parent contribution fees	1000 - 1200 points (weighted)	Gift voucher	700 - 900 points
Field trip vouchers	150 - 300 points	Family spa voucher	1500 - 1800 points
Family movie passes	500 - 700 points	School paraphernalia	200 - 400 points
Family weekend get-a-ways	1500 - 1800 points	Family dining with the minister - Social media post	1500 - 1800 points
Swim passes	50 - 100 points	Tickets to national festivals	500 - 700 points
Family picnic passes	500 - 700 points	Tickets to national sporting events	500 - 700 points
Internet access plans	300 - 450 points	Exit examination fees grant	2000 points

Table 8
Home Support Home-Based Incentive Program

Categories of home support engagements	Sample activities	Points plan
Parenting	Parenting seminar (face to face, virtual – synchronous or asynchronous, participation in blogs or online forums etc.).	10 points
	Parenting support teams/family support programs (traditional or virtual) 10 points	
	Students attend school at least 85% of the time	10 points per term
	Student punctual at least 90% of time	10 points per term
	Student appropriately attired at least 80% of the time	10 points per term
	Student home work is done at least 95% of the time	15 points per term
	Student has all school supplies	15 points per term
	Student involved in at least one extra-curricular activity	15 points
	Student received 0% sanction for indiscipline	50 points
	Student representing the school nationally or internationally	100 points
	Student earned recognition for areas of excellence (academics, leadership, sports, arts etc.)	100 points
Communicating	Attendance to PTA (traditional or virtual)	10 points each
	Attendance to parent teacher conferences (traditional or virtual)	20 points each
	Timetabled weekly parent conferences (traditional or virtual)	5 points each
	Prize-giving ceremonies (traditional or virtual)	10 points each
	Registered on the text messaging system	2 points
	Visit to the school website	2 points
	Sign up on the email messaging system	2 points
	Participate in forums	10 points each
	Participate in the class WhatsApp group	5 points
	Access the school management database	20 points per term
	Attendance to monthly class meeting (traditional or virtual)	10 points each
	Attendance to termly year group meeting (traditional or virtual)	10 points per term
	Attendance to weekly principal parent conference (traditional or virtual)	5 points each
	Written feedback to teachers on students work (printed or electronic)	5 points per ter
	Provide feedback on school policies and programs	10 points per term
	Provide feedback on notices, newsletters etc.	5 points per term
Volunteering	Member of the PTA executive/other committees (fundraising etc.)	20 points
	Lead implementer of any home support activity	15 points
	Managers of clubs and societies	15 points each
	Attendance to fundraising/other activities	10 points
	Volunteer Teacher/Presenter	20 points
	Class/Year Group Representative	20 points

SECTION 3: THE PROJECT

Home Support Home-Based Incentive Program - Part 2

Categories of home support engagements	Sample activities	Points plan
Learning at Home	Parent signature on homework	15 points
	Homework timetable established by parent and child (printed or shared in Google Docs)	5 points
	Parent collect curriculum guide/access online guide	15 points
	Parent submits monitoring feedback on curriculum guide (written or electronic through Google Doc, etc.)	15 points per term
	Study imetable established by parent and child (written or electronic through Google Doc, etc.)	5 points
	Parent and student are members of a library (online library accepted)	15 points
	Students attend extra classes	5 points per term
	Parent and student engage in research on subject content (shared written or electronic through Google Doc, etc.)	20 points per term
	Submits a calendar of activities for parents and student at home, with signed feedback from parent and student	20 points per term
	Parents attends curriculum review sessions (face to face or virtually)	10 points per term
	Student annual career plan with established parent support signed by both student and parent (shared written or electronic)	20 points
	Parent led intervention based on student needs	15 points
	Summer learning activities	20 points
Decision Making	Member of the school board	25 points
	Member of the school improvement plan committee	15 points
	Member of the school rules committee	15 points
	Member of the disciplinary committee	15 points
	Establish networks to link parents to lead representatives	10 points
	Member on community councils/advocacy group	10 points
Collaboration	Support community businesses	5 points
	Attend meeting with the community. Meet the community face-to-face or virtually)	20 points
	Member of the past student association	10 points
	Facilitate internship/apprenticeship for students	30 points
	Facilitate student volunteer programs in the community	30 points
	Serve as a mentor (traditionally or virtually)	10 points per term
	Offer special funding support for projects, etc.	60 points
	Pay agreed Parental Contribution annually	30 points
	Provided resources for school development (kind)	30 points
	Participate in school-community projects	30 points
	Provide expert service in school community projects like health fairs, beautification projects, etc.	30 points
	Share information on community activities (face-to-face or virtually)	10 points

The leadership of the school, leadership of the PTA, and the Ministry of Education officials/designate will form the planning and monitoring committee. This committee will first convene a planning meeting to discuss the program tenets as outlined above. An individual should also be invited to the meeting to record the minutes. This meeting should be convened by the end of May to allow for adequate time for the full implementation in September, when the new academic year begins. The meeting may be chaired by the principal and be guided by the agenda below:

Proposed Agenda of Planning Meeting

Call to Order – Chairperson (Principal)
Prayer
Welcome
Introductions
- Overview of the state of parent involvement at the school
- Overview of the incentivized parent engagement program
- Discussion on the value of the program to school development
- Discussion on the components of the program applicable to the school
- Decision on the suggested components of the program to be implemented in the school with modifications where necessary
- Decision on the wider stakeholder consultation – date, time, venue and who will coordinate the activities for the hosting of the stakeholders' consultations.

Closing remarks
Termination

Figure 6. Proposed agenda of planning meeting

A consultation session will then be convened with the teachers and parents separately and guided by the agenda outlined above. The overview of the program will be presented to each stakeholder group as well as the suggested program of the committee. The proposed changes, if any, will be recorded and the modified program drafted, demonstrating the school-based, home-based and school home-based engagements which will form a part of the home-support program that the school will operate. This could reflect the program as designed in the description above or reflect other activities according to school size, location and other contextual factors. One volunteer from the group of teachers and one from the parents will be coopted to the planning committee. They will revise the plan and this draft will then be presented to the teachers and parents for ratification at the second consultation meeting. The ratified document will then be presented to the board of management for further ratification by the end of June of the academic year. Once this is ratified by all stakeholders, a report on the policy implementation tenets should be sent to the Ministry of Education to support the request for funding using the parent involvement premium. The policy tenets should also be sent to the PTA, so that it can be used to commit funding to finance and sustain the incentive component of the policy.

Implementation Plan – Stage 2: Crafting the Budget

Following the ratification of the board of management, the planning team (principal, PTA representative, and the Ministry representative) should meet to craft a budget which should be funded by the school, Ministry of Education and the PTA. In the Jamaican context, schools are allowed to generate income from canteen/tuck shop sales among other ventures. The PTA is allowed to collect financial contribution from the parents as well as to host fundraisers to support the activities of the PTA or the programs of the school. The annual contribution may range from JD$500.00 to $3,500.00. The Ministry of Education would also provide support, based on the proposed parent involvement premium of JD$2,000. Therefore, a school with a total of 500 students could realize an annual income and expenditure for the parent engagement program as outlined in Figure 7.

Implementation Plan – Stage 3: Organizing the Systems

Following ratification by the board of management and the crafting of the budget, the principal will ensure that the crafted program is sent to the Ministry of Education to support the request for funding using the parent involvement premium. The PTA will also receive a copy of the program plan to which it will commit funding support to finance and sustain the incentive component of the program as well as further sensitize parents of agreed expectations. The principal will also share a copy with teachers so that their roles are fully understood in the implementation of the program.

	BUDGET		
Income	**$JD**	**Expenditures**	**$JD**
Funding from Ministry of Education (500 students x $2,000)	1,000,000	Salary – administrator	264,000
Funding from the PTA (500 students x $1,000)	500,000	Computer system	60,000
Funding from school (500 students x $1,500)	750,000	Stationeries	70,000
Administration support (Apprenticeship program - MoE)	264,000	SMS/texting system	150,000
		Office maintenance	150,000
		Learning management system	100,000
		Virtual learning environment	70,000
		Multimedia devices	500,000
		Incentives	1,000,000
		Miscellaneous	150,000
Total	**2,514,000**	**Total**	**2,514,000**

Figure 7. Parent involvement premium for a school with 500 students enrolled

SECTION 3: THE PROJECT

Based on the budget, the principal will procure the resources required for their implementation based on school context or needs. The following resources will be needed, if the school is not already in possession of same:

- A parent support office – the data entry clerk will operate from this office
- Stationeries
- Office computer
- Internet access
- SMS system
- Text messaging communication plan
- Virtual Learning Environment – online forums, conferences
- Learning Management System; document sharing applications
- Multimedia devices, cameras, speakers, recorders, and so on.
- Websites/social media/online calendar/online noticeboards
- Meeting rooms for PTA meeting and conferences
- Agreed incentives

The data entry clerk must be competent in the use of information communication technological devices and will be required to set up online facilities as outlined in the program design. The data entry clerk will use data gathered from teachers, online activities, disciplinary records, and the registers for face-to-face activities, such as conferences or meetings, to determine who earned points and the number of points earned. When parents earn points, an electronic chip or a written note will be sent to notify them of points earned and the equivalent incentives in the event that they would like to redeem their points. Parents, however, will have the opportunity to accumulate points up to 5 years (duration of secondary education) to earn incentives of greater value.

The principal will present the assessment plan and the school's calendar to the data entry clerk so that a schedule for data collection can be developed as well as provide access to monthly attendance records. The PTA will also present to the data entry clerk the calendar of activities and attendance records after each activity, so that those who earn points can be determined. The data entry clerk will use this information to generate the data to support the award of points for all activities. The clerk will subsequently furnish a monthly report to the principal and the PTA president and a termly report to the Ministry of Education. The clerk will distribute daily or monthly incentives or as they are claimed by parents using the incentives claim form seen on the following page. The principal and the PTA executive will use the reports to determine the class and year group incentive awards, while the Ministry of Education will use the termly reports to determine the national home-school incentive awards.

The general interest in increased parental involvement and the shared understanding of its impact on the success of students and schools have created the enabling environment for a policy of this nature to be implemented. The potential societal impacts, such as reduced crime rate, improved literacy rate and a more educated citizenry, among others, are also supporting factors for the success of this policy. The fact that the policy calls for the involvement of school, home and state has implications for sustainability. The resources for a policy of this nature, however, may be expensive for a small school or a school that has limited funding. This can be addressed over time. The policy could be implemented in phases by only implementing a few activities at a time or scaling down the activities, then increasing them annually. Also, the incentives could be changed to more affordable items through collective agreement. The employment of a data entry clerk might be expensive for small schools; however, this could be addressed by using volunteers in the form of past students and current students through a service learning program or community representatives. Also, requesting a clerk through the government's apprenticeship program could be another option, as well as designing the portfolio as a senior teacher post and requesting that the government provides the stipend for same.

SECTION 3: THE PROJECT

Home School Engagement Incentives Claim Form

I ....parent of ....of class .... have

earned.........points and would like to redeem these points for the

following incentive(s)..

....
Parent's Signature   Data Entry Clerk's Signature

....
Principal's Signature

Figure 8. Home school engagement incentives claim form

Implementation Plan – Stage 4: Launch of the Program

The planning committee will meet to plan the date, time and venue of the launch of the program. This will be done annually to ensure that the program remains a central activity in the school and should take place at a general assembly, where students, the principal, teachers, parents and the Ministry of Education representatives are in attendance. The program should commence on the first Monday of the school year and end on the last Friday in the academic year (first Monday in September – the first Friday in July).

Implementation Plan – Stage 5: Policy Monitoring and Evaluation

According to Lodico et al. (2010), program evaluation is a process that redounds to an overall assessment of a program to identify its strengths, weaknesses and impact and to proffering of recommendations for programmatic improvement and greater success. For the purposes of this program, the objective based approach will be utilized. The objective based approach uses written objectives by both the creators of the program and the evaluators to determine if the program is successful as guided by the program's benchmarks (Lodico et al., 2010). In other words, formative and summative data will be collected and compared with the program's objectives, which were used in shaping the evaluation.

In executing this objective-based evaluation, the data will be captured using an audit template focused on key home-school engagements. An audit of the engagements will be captured before, during and at the end of the program each year. This data will be captured from the principal, a sample of teachers and parents. A comparative analysis will be done to determine the impact of the program on each variable of interest. Where there are increases in each area of interest, this will be interpreted as a positive outcome of the program. Where there are no changes or a decline in the variable, a recommendation will be made to change the activities and implement others, which may have a more positive impact on the variables of interest. The form outlined in Figure 9 will be used to collate the data.

The monthly reports generated by the data entry clerk as well as the parent incentive claim forms should be used by the planning/monitoring committee to monitor the success of the program during the academic year. This data gathered can be used to determine if modifications, resensitization, promotion, among other changes, are necessary as the program progresses. The formative assessment, monitoring and summative reports will be used by the planning/monitoring committee with the help of the data entry clerk to generate an end of year report of the program.

Implementation Plan - Stage 6: Celebrations and Awards

Using the monitoring and evaluation report, the planning committee will plan and host a celebration and awards event to highlight the successes of the program and its impact on the school. The planning and execution can be guided by the program outlined in Figure 10.

SECTION 3: THE PROJECT

Home Support Engagement Program Evaluation Form

Program Goal: To increase the involvement of parents in home support engagements, thereby, improving students' outcomes and by extension the school's performance.

Formative/Summative Data

	Responses	Comments	Variances
Does the school operate an active PTA?			
What is the average attendance at a PTA?			
What is the average attendance at a Parent Seminar?			
What is the average attendance at a Parent Teacher Conference?			
What percentage of the student population is adequately prepared for school (decorum and school supplies)?			
What percentage of the student population is punctual for school?			
What is the home work submission rate?			
What percentage of the student population is involved in extracurricular activities?			
How many parent volunteers do you have?			
What is the suspension/expulsion rate for students?			
What percentage of students' performs above the pass rate of your institution?			
How many opportunities for two-way communication exist in your school?			
How many opportunities for community collaboration exist in your school?			
How many opportunities for parent involvement in decision making exist in your school?			
How many opportunities to enable parents to support student learning at home exist in your school?			
What percentage of parents gives resources towards school projects or programs?			

Figure 9. Home support engagement program evaluation form

Home School Incentive Program
Celebrations and Awards Function

Musical Interlude	
Opening Prayer	School Chaplain
Welcome	Chairman of the Board
Opening Remarks	Moderator
Program Overview	Principal
Greetings	Ministry of Education Representatives
	Parent Teachers' Association
Item	School Choir
Presentation of Awards	
	Parent and Student of the Year (most points earned)
	Class/Form of the Year (most points earned by a class)
	Year Group of the Year (most points earned by a year group)
	School of the Education Region (most points earned by a school within a Region)
	School of the Year (school that earns the most points nationally)
Closing Remarks	
Refreshment	

Figure 10. Home school incentive award program

POLICY IMPLICATIONS

Home support for students learning can be considered vital to realizing social change within a society (Reeler, 2015). Reeler further adds, "social or individual change is not a cause and effect response, but is the release of the inner and outer constraints that hold persons in a particular state" (p. 16). If persons can be supported to move those constraints, then they can move themselves to paths of success (Reeler, 2015). This policy seeks to enable partnership between home and school to support the educational and future successes of students. In so doing, this will help to remove the social, economic, educational and psychological constraints, which prevent students from taking advantage of opportunities or from making developmental choices (Bennett-Conroy, 2012).

The improved practices to be garnered from this policy could realise improvements in student, parent and teacher motivation, and a reduction in the gaps in teaching pedagogy, teaching time, resource allocation, and the constraints that parents face in balancing parenting and work responsibilities. The united efforts of parents and school personnel could result in the shared interest for student success being channelled appropriately through targeted activities, which could provide additional resources to support students learning, such as the incentives component of the program. Students' self efficacy may also improve with improved academic performance and increased interaction with their parents. The parent-child relationship could also improve from parents showing and doing more for their children through their participation in the engagements, resulting in a tighter family bond. This policy also acknowledges and builds on the assets that parents bring to educational partnerships and posits a standardised system-wide approach to parent involvement, with flexibility for modification according to school context and capacity.

Teachers tend to be more motivated to help students where their parents show interest in them. This policy seeks to elicit more involvement and, thus, teachers will be motivated to teach and give extra time to ensure student mastery. With a motivated staff and student body, then improved performance academically is anticipated for all students. This will further result in improvement in school performance and school image, thereby, building students allegiance and their potential to give back to school development efforts after graduation. This could also mean greater past student support from the local bodies and those who are a part of the diaspora community for education.

If parental involvement improves at the school level, then parents' involvement in the National PTA could also improve. This could realise increased participation in national activities for parent and school development. The National Parenting Support Commission, which is set up by the government of Jamaica to coordinate all national parenting support activities, could benefit from this framework, in that their use of it could strengthen their presence and relevance. This policy also provides a framework for government to increase its funding of education and to demonstrate the value it places on parents' involvement in their children's education. The government could also pitch this as a school-based social intervention policy aimed at reducing youth delinquency and criminal activities within the wider society. The NEI stands also to benefit from this framework as use of it could also strengthen their evaluation instrument of parenting support in education. In general, this policy has the potential to become an international best practice and a guide for future research, which could be of major social significance and importance to the improvement of the wider education sector.

Section 4:
Reflection

REFLECTION

The information gleaned from the participants in this study was profound. The information revealed that each stakeholder group wanted each child, being the nucleus of the education system, to succeed; the success of students meant different things to each stakeholder and the varying meanings provided the motivation for involvement. There were some categories of activities that were more important to parents: communication, decision making, volunteering and parenting. There was a need to utilize technology in incorporating the motivations of parents to be involved and in remediating the challenges that thwart parental support. This knowledge is important since many school leaders sometimes assume that parents do not care about their children as much as they should and that too much was left for the school to do. When you observe the expressed challenges that prevent parent involvement in schools, it is evident that more needed to be done to enable home-school partnerships and that home-school partnerships required creativity in design in order to generate greater involvement, accountability and impact. The strategic utility of the findings of this study could, therefore, assist in the creation of home-support engagement programs, which could remove the constraints impeding the performance of students and schools and guide them into success, which is the epitome of social change.

Project Strengths

The data gleaned from this study were used to draft a policy that could be used to support the redefinition and incentivization of home-support engagements aimed at improved student performance in the Jamaican education system. This policy encapsulates the motivations that influenced the stakeholders' involvement and the suggestions given to remedy the challenges that prevented the parents from being more involved. This policy presented several strengths from which the education sector could benefit. Firstly, the policy was informed by the stakeholders themselves. If an initiative is to benefit a particular group, it is always best to let the group inform its development so that it will reflect their context and address their situation more definitively (Martin & Pear, 2016). This policy, therefore, has the potential to increase home-school engagements, as it incorporated the ideas, needs, motivations and the challenges faced by affected stakeholders.

Secondly, this policy represents a guide that educators and parents alike can use to develop or modify home support engagements in their schools. In so doing, they could use it as an evaluation tool as well as to introduce new benchmarks, which could improve the program in operation. By using the policy tenets as an evaluation tool, stakeholders will be able to identify strengths and weaknesses in the programs and use this information to support their program improvement plans. Thirdly, the policy, though descriptive in its present form, allows for flexibility and individuality. The data reflect that school contexts are different and, therefore, stakeholders may modify the policy design to match their contexts or use sections of it until they can institute the complete policy. Fourthly, it can be used by the National PTA, the National Parenting Support Commission and the NEI, all of which have an interest in parents' inclusion in education to strengthen their work with schools and parents. The National PTA could use the policy document to set up home-support programs in schools as well as to design their national award program for schools that demonstrate a culture of parental inclusion. The National Parenting Support Commission could use the policy to guide aspects of the operational activities for their established parent places in schools and communities. Personnel of the parent places could be the candidates for the implementing and monitoring of the home-support activities in schools and at homes. The NEI could use the findings from the research and the policy to modify its school inspection instrument, especially the section that measures parental involvement. This could measure the specifics within a school and give credence to the school context and plans, rather than a generic expectation.

Fifthly, the policy offers an opportunity for home, school and state to work in tandem to ensure greater student outcomes. Instead of each entity embarking on a discrete program, this policy presents the opportunity for the merger of resources towards a common cause, which may be better sustained with a tripartite partnership. It also professes inclusivity for all stakeholders, as each group is catered for and given a valued place in the partnership for student success. Sixthly, the policy is grounded in research, thereby, incorporating the principles of reinforcements/incentives/rewards and the categories of parental involvement. This provides confidence in the tenets of the policy, and gives credibility to its proposed impacts. Finally, the policy is economical and can be easily integrated in the school system. Most of the required resources are already in most schools and where they are not, they can be procured incrementally while the other aspects of the policy are being implemented.

Project Limitations

Notwithstanding the strengths of this policy, there are some limitations. Based on the design of the policy, it is evident that its success is dependent on a partnership between home, school and state. Where it is difficult to obtain the commitment of one or two of the listed stakeholders, the potential benefits might be thwarted or delayed. Success is also dependent on the acceptance, uptake and adherence to the policy components. Some parents might not be willing to accept incentives for doing their job as parents, while others might over-engage at the expense of their other parental duties. Some parents might start out well in the program but might not adhere to the tenets and eventually lose interest. The policy could also create conflict in the school-home component where incentives are dependent on the collective participation of all the parents within a year group or the wider school population. The greater the number of parents involved, the greater the chances to earn incentives; the fewer parents involved, the greater the likelihood of conflict between those who participated and those who are uninterested. The policy also requires the support of someone who has expertise in the use of technology, who appreciates working with data, and who has good relationship skills, since they will have to interact with all stakeholder groups. Not finding someone with the right fit for the program could compromise quality and intended outcomes.

Overall, this study has added to the body of research on home-school engagement and has shown support for its importance in achieving equity and quality in the education program. It was found that schools with strong parent involvement programs were more successful than those with little or none and likewise the children. Though each stakeholder had various factors influencing their involvement such as their beliefs, the benefits, the ability of their children, among others, it is of benefit to infuse the motivational factors that inspire parents to participate in the schooling of their children in the design of home school engagement programs. It has shown also that all stakeholders are interested in the success of the students in their charge and though they are challenged by time, the lack of spousal support, among other factors, their involvement could be enabled by the use of information and communication technology. Activities which support parents' involvement in communication, decision making, volunteering and parenting, were found to be most important to the respondents and thus could be used as a guide to develop a minimum standard in parent involvement programs which may be critical in the quest to address the achievement gaps of our children.

SECTION 4: REFLECTION

RECOMMENDATIONS

Enacting a legislative framework for parental involvement is highly recommended as the catalyst for change and inclusion of home school engagement in education. In an effort to strengthen and sustain the impact of the legislative changes, funding of parental involvement programs is one such extra school support that should increase as a global practice. One method of implementation of this practice is through the incentivization of home support engagements. As found from this research, parents have the expressed desire to be involved in the educational activities of their children, but this is sometimes made difficult due to work demands, lack of spousal support and financial challenges. Instead of a focus on traditional approach that privileges a few, a collaborative design model is encouraged. Compensating schools for parental engagement posits a transformative potential as a starting point for more meaningful and authentic educational policy dialogues.

Parenting programs buffered by incentives could leverage greater home-school partnerships, as when offered together, they have the potential to elicit desired home-school engagement behaviors and attitude. In this approach, parents earn tokens for each parent support activity that they engage in which may be exchanged for school-related benefits for their children. As a consequence, parents could learn skills to support their children's education and possibly inspire closer family ties and permanent change in behavior. This incentivized home-school engagement program should include the 6 categories of engagements: parenting, communicating, volunteering, learning at home, decision making and collaborating as proposed by Epstein (2001). It also may include a minimum number of activities under each category and reflect the following 3 components: school-based, home-based and school and home-based tenets. While some critics might advocate against this move, on the basis that it may present as a bribe to get parent to perform their jobs, the possibility exists that if executed appropriately, incentivizing home-school engagements has the potential to elicit desired behaviors thereby providing the enablement that could increase the educational outcomes and life chances of our students.

Another recommendation that may sustain the parent involvement efforts in education transformation is the practice of school and parents cocreating a shared home-school engagement program that reflects the uniqueness of the parents and the lifestyle challenges faced by them. One method that has the potential to respond to the uniqueness of families is the incorporation of contemporary tools to foster greater home-support involvement. Given the challenges of work demands and lack of spousal support faced by families, the traditional approach of face-to-face encounters for parents has proven limiting. We are currently in the information communication technological era and thus this wave of technological improvement could be incorporated in parent involvement efforts to respond to the needs of those not privileged by the traditional mode.

The newly embraced hybrid model to teaching and learning could be replicated in the cascading efforts of the school, home and state to increase and improve parent involvement in education. Each school may need to evaluate its parent involvement plan and utilize the available technological devices to cocreate an improvement plan. The communication between home and school can be drastically improved with applications such as WhatsApp, SMS, learning management systems, Google Docs, Zoom, Skype, teleconferencing among others. Parents can make their voices be heard in decisions of the school by completing online surveys, participating in online fora or even through emails. Parenting conferencing can be participated in asynchronously to build parents capacities to be effective parents. The fact is, the opportunities generated by technology inclusion are limitless, can be tailored by context and thus should be explored for the benefit of our students and by extension, nation building. It must be noted that the quantity of opportunities generated from the technology inclusion should reflect the uniqueness and interest of the diversity in the school community, and efforts should be exerted to maintain the quality of the opportunities for parent involvement.

SECTION 4: REFLECTION

Since the ranking of schools based on their academic performance triggers widened interest in schools and motivates school personnel to improve their performance for higher rankings, it is further recommended that a similar approach be used on the parent involvement tenet. Due to the fluidity surrounding the definition of parent involvement, in the implementation of this recommendation, each state would need to agree on a common definition of home-school engagement and devise a method of evaluation based on the shared meaning. This data should then be used to rank schools and celebrate their efforts at parent inclusion and the attendant benefits. It is hoped that school managers and other stakeholders would be more consistent since the reputation of an institution is paramount and is worth protecting as explained by the respondents in this study.

Similar to the established patterns of countries developing a school improvement manual as a guide for schools, a parent engagement manual could be developed and circulated among schools. The cultures and subcultures of a country impact how parents view their roles at schools and thus, it would be wise for the government through the parent engagement manual, to provide opportunities for parents to be sensitized bout the developmental goals of education and their impacts on local needs as well as how they can participate in the realization of such goals through their involvement. More genuine and authentic forms of engagements have the potential to not only transform schools, but also the community that it serves and thus providing a guide has value and could counter the segregated views and approaches of homes and schools. Also, by the utility of this guide, where the evidence is provided showing a neglect of parents ard or school with respect to agreed expectations of parent engagement, the government should provide social support to modify this behavior as a means of ensuring that the child is provided with the greatest chance of success.

It is being recommended also that there should be a national parent teacher association and a parenting commission in all countries providing guidance to parents and supporting the successful implementation of home-support engagements at the local level. The school-based parent teachers association could submit their calendar of activities and termly report to these oversight bodies and they in turn should provide national support in the form of funding, resource personnel, publicity and commendations among others, to ensure the successful execution of these activities. Home-school engagement is undoubtedly a pillar of transformation that should be fully explored in context and collaboratively as part of the thrust to reduce the attainment gap thereby increasing the success chances of all students.

References

Abel, Y. (2012). African American fathers' involvement in their children's school-based lives. Journal of Negro Education, 81(2), 162-172.

Adamski, A., Fraser, B., & Peiro, M. (2013). Parental involvement in schooling, classroom environment and student outcomes. Learning Environments Research, 16, 315–328. doi:10.1007/s10984-012-9121-7

Ambrosio, J. (2013). Changing the subject: Neoliberalism and accountability in public education. Education Studies, 49, 316-333. doi:10.1080/00131946.2013.783835

Angus, G. (2016, February 11). New national standards curriculum for 2016/17 school year. The Jamaica Information Services. Retrieved from http://jis.gov.jm/new-national-standards-curriculum-for-201617-school-year/

Baek, J., & Bullock, L. (2015). Evidence-based parental involvement programs in the United States of America and Korea. Journal of Child and Family Studies, 24(6), 1544-1550. doi:10.1007/s10826-014-9958-8

Bennett-Conroy, W. (2012). Engaging parents of eighth grade students in parent-teacher bidirectional communication. School Community Journal, 22(2), 87-110.

Bogdan, R. C., & Biklen, S. K. (2007). Qualitative research for education: An introduction to theories and methods (5th ed.). Boston, MA: Allyn & Bacon.

Bracke, D., & Cort, D. (2012). Parental involvement and the theory of planned behaviour. Education, 133(1), 188-201.

Brown, C. (2013). Phronetic expertise in evidence use: A new perspective on how research can aid educational policy development. Prometheus, 31(3), 189–203. doi:10.1080/08109028.2013.850186

Caribbean Policy Research Institute. (2009). Improving Jamaica's education: Options for using report cards to measure performance and improve accountability. Kingston, Jamaica: Author.

Cavanagh, S. (2012). Parental engagement proves no easy goal. Education Week, 31(27), 16-17.

Cooper, C. W. (2009). Parent involvement, African American mothers, and the politics of educational care. Equity & Excellence in Education, 42(4), 379-394.

Creswell, J.W. (2009). Research design: Qualitative, quantitative, and mixed methods approaches (3rd ed.). Thousand Oaks, CA: Sage Publication.

Creswell, J. W. (2012). Educational research: Planning, conducting, and evaluating quantitative and qualitative research. Boston, MA: Pearson.

Davis, R. (2004). Task force on educational reform Jamaica. A transformed education system 2004 report. Retrieved from http://jis.gov.jm/estp/docs/Reports/JA%20Education%20Reform%20TaskForce%202004.pdf

Dee, T. S. (2011). Conditional cash penalties in education: Evidence from the learnfare experiment. Economics of Education Review, 30, 924-937.

Dwyer, M. (2013). National education inspectorate chief inspector report. Kingston, Jamaica: Ministry of Education.

Epstein, J. L. (1995). School/family/community partnerships: Caring for the children we share. Phi Delta Kappan, 76(9), 701-712.

REFERENCES

Epstein, J. L. (1996). Perspectives and previews on research and policy for school, family, and community partnerships. In A. Booth & J. F. Dunn (Eds.), Family-school links: How do they affect educational outcomes? (pp. 209-246). Mahwah, NJ: Erlbaum.

Epstein, J. L. (2001). School, family, and community partnerships. Boulder, CO: Westview Press.

Epstein, J. L., Sanders, M. G., Simon, B.S., Salina, K.C., Jansorn, N.R., & Van Voorhis, F. L. (2002). School, family, and community partnerships: Your handbook for action (2nd ed.). Thousand Oaks, CA: Corwin Press, Inc.

Epstein, J. L. (2005). Developing and sustaining research-based programs of school family and community partnerships: Summary of five years of research. Baltimore, Maryland: The Center on School, Family and Community Partnerships at Johns Hopkins University.

Epstein, J. L. (2011). School, family, and community partnerships: Preparing educators and improving schools (2nd ed.). Philadelphia, PA: Westview Press.

Epstein, J. L. (2014). Joyce Epstein school-family-community partnership model. Research Starters Education, 1-8.

Fan, X., & Chen, M. (2001). Parental involvement and students' academic achievement: A meta-analysis. Educational Psychology Review, 13(1), 1-22. doi:10.1023/A:1009048817385

Fantuzzo, J. W., Tighe, E., & Childs, S. (2000). Family involvement questionnaire: A multivariate assessment of family participation in early childhood education. Journal of Educational Psychology, 92, 367-376.

Fryer Jr, R. G., Levitt, S. D., & List, J. A. (2015). Parental incentives and early childhood achievement: A field experiment in Chicago Heights. National Bureau of Economic Research.

Gerhart, B., & Fang, M. (2014). Pay for (individual) performance: Issues, claims, evidence, and the role of sorting effects. Human Resource Management Review 24, 41–52.

Giles, E., Robalino, S., Sniehotta, F., & Adams, J. (2014). Systematic review, meta-analysis and metaregression of the effectiveness of financial incentives for encouraging healthy behaviours. PLoS ONE, 9(3).

Giles, E., Robalino, S., Sniehotta, F., Adams, J., & McColl, E. (2015). Acceptability of financial incentives for encouraging uptake of healthy behaviours: A critical review using systematic methods. Prev Med. doi:10.1016/j.ypmed.2014.12.029.

Gillies, D. (2014). Knowledge activism: Bridging the research/policy divide. Critical Studies in Education, 55(3), 272–288. doi:/10.1080/17508487.2014.919942

Goodall, J., & Montgomery, C. (2014). Parental involvement to parental engagement: A continuum. Educational Review, 66(4), 399-410. doi:10.1080/00131911.2013.781576

Goodman, F., & Turner, T. (2013). The design of teacher incentive pay and educational outcomes: Evidence from the New York City bonus program. Journal of Labor Economics, 31(2), 409-420.

Graves Jr, S. L. & Wright, L. B. (2011). Parent involvement at school entry: A national examination of group differences and achievement. School Psychology International, 32(1), 35-48.

Greene, E., Pack, A., Stanton, J., Shelus, V., Tolley, E., Taylor, J..., Gamble, T. (2017). "It makes you feel like someone cares" acceptability of a financial incentive intervention for HIV viral suppression in the HPTN 065 (TLC-Plus) study. PLoS ONE, 12(2), 1-18. doi:10.1371/journal.pone.0170686.

Hall, J., & Ryan, K. (2011). Educational accountability: A qualitatively driven mixed- methods approach. Qualitative Inquiry, 17(1), 105-117. doi:10.1177/1077800410389761

Hamilton, C. (2012, April 16). Schools struggling – Inspectorate reports dismal performances. The Jamaica Observer. Retrieved from http://m.jamaicaobserver.com/mobile/news/Schools-struggling

Hilgendorf, A. E. (2012). Through a limiting lens: Comparing student, parent, and Teacher perspectives of African American boys' support for school. School Community Journal, 22(2), 111-130.

REFERENCES

Hofstede, G. (1983). The cultural relativity of organizational practices and theories. Journal of International Business Studies, 14, 75-89.

Hoover–Dempsey, K. V., Walker, J. M. T., Sandler, H. M., Whetsel, D., Green, C. L., Wilkins, A. S., & Closson, K. E. (2005). Why do parents become involved? Elementary School Journal, 106(2), 105-130.

Hornby, G. (2000). Improving parental involvement. London, England: Cassell.

Hornby, G., & Lafaele, R. (2011). Barriers to parental involvement in education: An explanatory model, Educational Review, 63(1), 37-52, doi:10.1080/00131911.2010.488049

Isk-Ercan, Z. (2010). Looking at school from the house window: Learning from Turkish- American parents' experiences with early elementary education in the United States. Early Childhood Education Journal, 38(2), 133-142. doi:10.1007/sl0643-010-0399-8

Jeynes, W. H. (2012). A meta-analysis of the efficacy of different types of parental involvement programs for urban students. Urban Education, 47(4), 706-742.

Johnson, M. (2012). Evaluating cultures: The instrumentalism, pluralist, perfectionism, and particularism of John Grey. Educational Theory, 62(5), 553-572.

Kabir, A. H., & Akter, F. (2014). Parental involvement in the secondary schools in Bangladesh: Challenges and a way forward. International Journal of Whole Schooling, 10(1), 1-18.

Kohl, G. O., Lengua, L. J., & McMahon, R. J. (2000). Parent involvement in school: Conceptualizing multiple dimensions and their relations with family and demographic risk factors. Journal of School Psychology, 38, 501-523.

Kohn, A. (1993). Why incentive plans cannot work. Harvard Business Review, 71(5), 54-63.

Kurtulmus, Z. (2016). Analyzing parental involvement dimensions in early childhood education. Educational Research and Reviews, 11(12), 1149-1153. doi:10.5897/ERR2016.2757.

LaRocque, M., Kleiman, I., & Darling, S. M. (2011). Parental involvement: The missing link in school achievement. Preventing School Failure, 55(3), 115-122. doi:10.1080/10459880903472876

Levitt, S., List, J., Metcalfe, R., & Sadoff, S. (2016). Engaging parents in parent engagement programs. Society for Research on Educational Effectiveness.

Lim, M. (2012). Unpacking parent involvement: Korean American parents' collective networking. School Community Journal, 22(1), 109-189.

Lodico, M., Spaulding, D. T., & Voegtle, K. (2010). Methods in educational research: From theory to practice. (Laureate Education, Inc., custom ed.). San Francisco, CA: John Wiley & Sons, Inc.

Lund, J., & Shanklin, J. (2011). The impact of accountability on student performance in a secondary physical education badminton unit. Physical Educator, 210-220.

Malone, D. (2015). Culture: A potential challenge for parental involvement in schools. Delta Kappa Gamma Bulletin: International Journal for Professional Educators, 82(1), 14-18.

Martorell, P., Miller, T., Santibañez, L., & Augustine, C. (2016). Can incentives for parents and students change educational inputs? Experimental evidence from summer school. Economics of Education Review, 50, 113-156.

Maslow, A. H. (1943). A theory of human behavior. Psychological Review, 370-398.

McMahon, M. (2014). Parent involvement in school. Research Starters Education, 1-7.

McWilliam, R. A. (2015). Future of early intervention with infants and toddlers for whom typical experiences are not effective. Remedial and Special Education, 36(1), 33-38.

REFERENCES

Martin, G., & Pear, J. (2016). Behavior modification: What it is and how to do it. New York, USA: Routledge.

Merriam, S. (2009). Qualitative research: A guide to design and implementation. San Francisco, CA: Jossey-Bass.

Merrill, C., Devine, K., Brown, J., & Brown, R. (2010). Improving geometric and trigonometric knowledge and skills for high school mathematics teachers: A professional development partnership. Journal of Technology Studies, 36(2), 20-30.

Miles, M. B., Huberman, A. M., & Saldana, J. (2014). Qualitative data analysis: A method sourcebook. Thousand Oaks, CA: Sage Publication.

Ministry of Education. (2006). Ministry paper – Grade six achievement test. Kingston, Jamaica: Author.

Ministry of Education. (2010). National education policy 2010. Dhaka: Ministry of Education.

Ministry of Education. (2016). Secondary schools placement list. Unpublished manuscript. Kingston, Jamaica: Author.

Ministry of Education, Youth and Information. (2017). Changing the game: Energizing the wave of prosperity – Strengthening partnerships in education. Kingston, Jamaica: Author.

Ministry of Education Supplement for Staff. (2012). Education system transformation programme: Reforming, transforming, performing. Kingston, Jamaica: Author.

Murphy, S. (2002). The attitudes of Jamaican parents towards parent involvement in high school education. Retrieved from http://www2.uwstout.edu/content/lib/thesis/2002/2002murphys.pdf

National College for Educational Leadership, (2017). Preparing principals for effective school leadership. Kingston, Jamaica: Author.

National Education Inspectorate. (2008). Draft of inspection handbook. Kingston, Jamaica: Author.

National Education Inspectorate. (2014). Chief inspector's report: Promoting excellence through quality inspections. Kingston, Jamaica: Author.

Okeke, C. (2014). Effective home-school partnership: Some strategies to help strengthen parental involvement. South African Journal of Education, 34(3), 1-9.

Olibie, E. (2014). Parental involvement in curriculum implementation as perceived by Nigeria secondary school principals. Journal of Education and Learning, 3(1), 40-51.

Otter, C. (2014). Family resources and mid-life level of education: A longitudinal study of the mediating influence of childhood parental involvement. British Educational Research Journal, 40(3), 555-574. doi:10.1002/berj.3111

Pakter, A., & Chen, L. (2012). The daily text: Increasing parental involvement in education with mobile text messaging. Journal of Educational Technology Systems, 41(4), 353-367.

Parke, H., Ashcroft, R., Brown, R., Marteau, T. M., & Seale, C. (2013). Financial incentives to encourage healthy behaviour: An analysis of UK media coverage. Health Expectations: An International Journal of Public Participation in Health Care & Health Policy. 16(3), 292-304.

Partnership for Educational Revitalization in the Americas & Caribbean Policy Research Institute. (2012). A summary of prisms of possibility: A report card on education in Jamaica. Kingston, Jamaica: Author.

Pasco, D. (2013). The potential of using virtual reality technology in physical activity settings. Quest, 65, 429–441. doi:10.1080/00336297.2013.795906

Puryear, J. M., & Moodey, L. (2007). Accountability rare in Latin American Schools. Viewpoints Americas, 7(5), 1-3.

Reece, C., Staudt, M., & Ogle, A. (2013). Lessons learned from a neighborhood-based collaboration to increase parent engagement. School Community Journal, 23(2), 207-225.

Reeler, D. (2015). Exploring the real world of social change: Seven questions that keep us awake. OD Practitioner, 47(1), 15-24.

REFERENCES

Reynolds, A. (2008, May 26). National parent-teachers' association of Jamaica – Boosting education through parent involvement. Jamaica Gleaner. Retrieved from http://old.jamaica-gleaner.com/gleaner/20080526/lead/lead6.html

Ross, T. (2016). The differential effects of parental involvement on high school completion and postsecondary attendance. Education Policy Analysis Archives, 24 (30), page number

Santana, L., Rothstein, D., & Bain, A. (2016). Partnering with parents to ask the right questions. Alexandria, VA: ASCD.

Semke, C. & Sheridan, S. (2012). Family-school connections in rural educational settings: A systematic review of the empirical literature. School Community Journal, 22(1), 21-47.

Shaw, J., & Gupta, N. (2015). Let the evidence speak again! Financial incentives are more effective than we thought. Human Resource Management Journal, 25(3), 281-293. doi:10.1111/1748-8583.12080

Sheng, X. (2012). Cultural capital and gender differences in parental involvement in children's schooling and higher education choice in China. Gender and Education, 24(2), 131-146.

Shumow, L., & Miller, J. D. (2001). Parents' at-home and at-school involvement with young adolescents. Journal of Early Adolescence, 21(1), 68-91. doi:10.1177/0272431601021001004

Speid, O. (2015, April 4). Act to rescue small schools. The Jamaica Observer. Retrieved From http://www.jamaicaobserver.com/columns/Act-to-rescue-small-schools_19220436

Thwaites, R. (2014). Sectoral presentation 2014-2015 student achievement. Kingston, Jamaica: Author. Retrieved from http://moe.gov.jm/sites/default/files/HMEsectoralD21%2 May7.pdf

Toper, D., Keane, S., Shelton, T., & Calkins, S. (2010). Parent involvement and student academic performance: A multiple mediational analysis. Journal of Prevention & Intervention in the Community, 38(3), 183-197. doi:10.1080/10852352.2010.486297

Tseng, V. (2012). The uses of research in policy and practice. Social Policy Report, 26(2), 1-16.

U.S. Department of Education. (n.d.). No Child Left Behind Act of 2001. Retrieved, from https://www.ed.gov/esea

Vega, D., Moore III, J., & Miranda, A. (2015). Who really cares? Urban youths' perceptions of parental and programmatic support. School Community Journal, 25 (1), 53-72.

Vygotsky, L. S. (1978). Mind and society: The development of higher mental processes. Cambridge, MA: Harvard University Press.

Walden Institutional Review Board Research Ethics Guide. (2014). MA. USA.

Wang, Y. (2015). A trend study of the influences of parental expectation, parental involvement and self-efficacy on the English academic achievement of Chinese eighth graders. International Education, 46-68.

Winton, S., & Evans, M. P. (2014). Challenging political spectacle through grassroots policy dialogues. Canadian Journal of Educational Administration and Policy, 156, 1-30.

Young, C., Austin, S., & Growe, R. (2013). Defining parental involvement: Perception of school administrators. Education, 133(3), 291-297.